FORGIVENESS AND RECONCILIATION

Retreat/ Group Companion
WORKBOOK

RICHARD T. CASE

To my wife, Linda, who has learned these great truths of forgiveness and then demonstrated them to me and all our family and friends in real life. She understands that forgiveness is critical to live a life of freedom; that she can get there 100 percent of the time—all the time; and that this is a gift of God and a heart issue between her and God—a separate issue from reconciliation. With forgiveness, she then has learned the truths of reconciliation—that this requires two parties dealing with truth together; and that if the other party is not willing to go to truth, she can live with not being reconciled—still living in forgiveness and freedom. She is a continual reminder of how this important element of life (perhaps one of the most important since we live in a world where people, even those close to us, will continually hurt and offend us) is to be received and experienced so we are never burdened or oppressed. She always lives in joy, and thus brings true joy to me as we walk with God together. A honor to experience this together, honey!

Acknowledgments

We wish to thank all of the leaders of our **Ministry: Living Waters—ABIDE Ministries!** These leaders daily and faithfully also have learned to receive and live out forgiveness/reconciliation—and together are always giving this away to others who are being called by God to receive release and freedom in this most critical area of life. Thank you all:

These leaders are:

Jake & Mary Beckel
Joe & Leigh Bogar
Rich & Janet Cocchiaro
Larry & Sherry Collet
David & Melissa Dunkel
Tom & Susanne Ewing
Rick & Kelly Ferris
Joel & Christina Gunn
Scott & Terry Hitchcock
Chris & Jaclyn Hoover
Rick & Nancy Hoover
Tad & Monica Jones
Ed & Becky Kobel
Don & Rachelle Light
Chris & Heidi May
Terry & Josephine Noetzel
Steve & Carolyn Van Ooteghem
Preston & Lynda Pitts
Dan & Kathy Rocconi
Bob & Keri Rockwell
John & Michelle Santaferraro
Allyson & Denny Weinberg
Neal & Kathy Weisenburger

FORGIVENESS AND RECONCILIATION: GROUP COMPANION WORKBOOK
PUBLISHED BY LIVING WATERS—ABIDE MINISTRIES
7615 Lemon Gulch Way
Castle Rock, CO 80108

Unless otherwise noted, all Scripture quotations are from the ESV® Bible (The Holy Bible, English Standard Version®), copyright © 2001 by Crossway Bibles, a publishing ministry of Good News Publishers. Used by permission. All rights reserved.

ISBN: 978-1-7360588-5-5
Copyright © 2024 by Richard T. Case.

All rights reserved. No part of this publication may be reproduced, distributed or transmitted in any form or by any means, including photocopying, recording, or other electronic or mechanical methods, without the prior written permission of the publisher.

Publisher's Cataloging-in-Publication data

Names:
Title:
Description: .
Identifiers: ISBN | LCCN
Subjects:

Printed in the United States of America 2024 — 2nd ed

TABLE OF CONTENTS

Introduction 1

Lesson One:
What Is Un-Forgiveness? What Contributes To It? 4

Lesson Two:
Why We Withhold Forgiveness? 16

Lesson Three:
What Is Forgiveness? (Part 1)? 24

Lesson Four:
What Is Forgiveness? (Part 2)? 36

Lesson Five:
What Is Reconciliation? (Part 1)? 52

Lesson Six:
What Is Reconciliation? (Part 2)? 72

Lesson Seven:
Ambassadors in Reconciliation 88

Lesson Eight:
Practical Ways of Reconciliation in a Variety of Situations 102

FOREGIVENESS AND RECONCILIATION

INTRODUCTION

INTRODUCTION

> "The problem with this un-forgiveness is that we are hurting only ourselves—our own soul—and the ability to enjoy our own life."

The lack of forgiveness and reconciliation within relationships is an issue nearly all people experience. My wife, Linda, and I have been conducting marriage retreats for the past 12 years. In each retreat, almost all of the couples are dealing with these very issues: forgiveness and reconciliation. Lack of forgiveness oftentimes becomes a standard or learned behavior between the husband and wife. But from there, the behavior will spill over into relationships with parents, siblings, children, friends, workers, bosses, etc. Why is this such a problem? Because a lack of forgiveness leads to further negativity. It is true that we all are surrounded by selfish people who hurt and manipulate us to merely obtain what they want, especially what they want us to do for them. As we experience such wounds, frustrations, and opposition, we naturally become angry and then proceed to struggle with what to do with the anger. That anger quickly begins hardening hearts and dissolving intimacy within relationships. We maintain our un-forgiveness because the other party has not admitted or confessed their wrongdoing to us, and therefore, we wait upon them to make things right. Since most people do not respond to wounds by resolving what they have done to us (and often lack the admission of what we have done to them) everyone continues operating in un-forgiveness.

The problem with this un-forgiveness is that we are hurting only ourselves—our own soul—and the ability to enjoy our own life. Over the years Linda and I have worked to bring healing to people's lives through the power of forgiveness. What has become clear to us in this ministry, however, is that there is great confusion between forgiveness and reconciliation. This course serves to explore the depths of these differences, offer Biblical truths that allow us to live in forgiveness, and then offer reconciliation to those around us. We also will describe how to maintain forgiveness when those around us are unwilling to reconcile.

Case in point: At one of our retreats, a woman expressed deep bitterness toward her father who first had oppressed her as a child and then rejected her as an adult. In fact, he had rejected the entire family after divorcing her mother. Like her, all of her siblings were estranged from their father. During the retreat, the woman processed God's call to forgiveness and offer of reconciliation. She worked through the Word of God until she received that which she so eagerly sought: forgiveness toward her father. Having

INTRODUCTION

experienced the release of forgiving her father, she wanted to share it with the rest of her family. She called each of her siblings and expressed to them the freedom she had so beautifully received. She even went further suggesting that each sibling work through the same process until they, too, fully embraced and received the same forgiveness God was calling them to accept and to extend. Sadly, though, all of her siblings declined and chose to remain enslaved to their bitterness. What her siblings couldn't see was that by choosing bitterness and refusing to forgive actually placed each of them in bondage. As we will see throughout this course, refusing to process un-forgiveness causes continued—but avoidable—pain and angst.

But her story didn't end there. After this precious lady had received forgiveness regarding her father, she then contacted him to offer reconciliation. Her father was pleased to hear from her and was willing to meet. Though he was not able to process much of her actual pain, they did reconcile at a surface level and each experienced and felt the freedom of having regained a lost relationship. Then, less than a week later, her father passed away. This dear lady praised God for the gift of truth and revelation of forgiveness, but also that she was given the opportunity and power to express her love toward her father before he died. Her siblings, on the other hand, chose not to face their bitterness and even added to it by becoming annoyed with the sister who worked to mend the relationship with the father. They continue to be burdened by the bitterness they have developed over the years and now that bitterness cannot be let go. Again, this course will show how we each can come to, receive, and welcome forgiveness regarding those who have hurt us, even when those who have hurt us have passed away, and there is no chance for reconciliation.

This woman's story is, unfortunately, not unique. Most of us have similar stories in our own lives and are living within various levels of un-forgiveness and some level of bitterness. As we will discover, the truth and revelation of God found in the Scriptures declares God's call to us: a call to forgive and to forgive 100 percent of the time. In the same way, God desires that each of us lives in utter and complete freedom, freedom that can only be obtained through forgiveness.

We also will earn that forgiveness does not equal reconciliation, because reconciliation takes two willing parties. While this may feel like a complicated endeavor, we eventually will come to understand the simplicity of our position in the reconciliation process—which always starts and ends with forgiveness.

LESSON 1:
WHAT IS UN-FORGIVENESS? WHAT CONTRIBUTES TO IT?

Why do you think the lack of forgiveness and reconciliation is so prevalent in our day?

How would you define the following?

Forgiveness:

___

Reconciliation:

___

> "Where there is no forgiveness, there is no trace of anything resembling a forgiven life, a forgiven person, the evidence of forgiveness, or the evidence of Christ."

How and why do we confuse the two?

___

LESSON 1:
WHAT IS UN-FORGIVENESS? WHAT CONTRIBUTES TO IT?

We will spend time in this study exploring "forgiveness and reconciliation," both of which impact every life and thus our true enjoyment of life. In these sessions, we will uncover:

1. What "un-forgiveness" is and what contributes to it.

2. Why we withhold forgiveness.

3. What forgiveness is.

4. What reconciliation is.

5. Practical ways of obtaining reconciliation in a variety of situations.

> **Define Un-forgiveness from the following verses:**
> **Read Romans 11:30-32.**
>
> [30] For just as you were at one time disobedient to God but now have received mercy because of their disobedience, [31] so they too have now been disobedient in order that by the mercy shown to you they also may now[a] receive mercy. [32] For God has consigned all to disobedience, that he may have mercy on all.

_____
_____
_____
_____
_____

LESSON 1:
WHAT IS UN-FORGIVENESS? WHAT CONTRIBUTES TO IT

Read the following Scriptures:

Is this a choice? Why or why not?

Read Ephesians 4:26-27.

[26] Be angry and do not sin; do not let the sun go down on your anger, [27] and give no opportunity to the devil.

_____
_____
_____
_____
_____

Read Isaiah 28:16-17.

[16] therefore thus says the Lord God,
"Behold, I am the one who has laid[a] as a foundation in Zion,
   a stone, a tested stone,
a precious cornerstone, of a sure foundation:
   'Whoever believes will not be in haste.'
[17] And I will make justice the line,
   and righteousness the plumb line;
and hail will sweep away the refuge of lies,
   and waters will overwhelm the shelter."

_____
_____
_____
_____
_____

LESSON 1:
WHAT IS UN-FORGIVENESS? WHAT CONTRIBUTES TO IT?

> "Do not be afraid or too stubborn to look at the darkest recesses of your heart. Those doors you refuse to open to others, fling those wide open to Jesus."

Process through the following until you receive clarity and understanding:

We encounter circumstances or people causing injustice every day. The anger and frustration that accompany each event is unique to the people associated with it and to the offense. In our experience, we have noticed that there are basically three differing levels at which humanity typically responds to wounds. These are: Minimal, Partial, and Complete. Let's take a look at each one.

1. **Minimal:** not withdrawn or harsh, can talk to the other person, can be in same room, but upset at some level. There is a strain in the relationship; it tends to be short, edgy, somewhat distant; sometimes dogmatic; different.

2. **Partial:** are separated today. Do not want to talk about it right now. Are mad. Do not want to deal with this person so separate, even if for while, because we have to be together later; is affecting my ability to relate to on a friendly, rationale level. Tend to stuff things further, not resolve, eventually develops roots of bitterness; but later, maybe even tomorrow, act as if things are fine. The relationship is somewhat strained and certainly different; but a new normal is established.

3. **Complete:** want nothing to do with this person now; cut off all communications. Are mad, and unless the other party apologizes, admits what they did was wrong, how they were hurtful, and works to correct the problem, you are not budging.

If you are like most people, you probably have an incredibly long list of harmful actions done and words said to you through the years. Unfortunately, this is not uncommon in today's world, but with the litany of wounds we experience, what necessitates the level at which we respond? Everything has to do with your wound: how it happened, by whom it happened, etc. The events that surround your hurt, everything about its environment, contribute to how we respond.

The level of the response is determined by:

1. **Severity of hurt**

2. **Frequency of hurt**

3. **Current level of frustration about other things:**

LESSON 1:
WHAT IS UN-FORGIVENESS? WHAT CONTRIBUTES TO IT?

- Tired, weary
- Worried, anxious
- Fear
- Roots of bitterness, anger
- Grief, sadness
- Disappointments, resignation

4. **Hardness, stubbornness of person hurting me**

5. **Emotional escalation of the moment:**

    - Words spoken that accuse; attack my character:

    - Circumstances that appear to deepen my hurt and anger—whether imagined or real:

    - Where the level stays is based upon our (and the other person's) current walk with God:

Walking in the Spirit: a righteous anger at injustice and being wronged:

> **Read Romans 12:9-21.**
> **Note here the marks of the true Christian.**
>
> [9] Let love be genuine. Abhor what is evil; hold fast to what is good. [10] Love one another with brotherly affection. Outdo one another in showing honor. [11] Do not be slothful in zeal, be fervent in spirit,[a] serve the Lord. [12] Rejoice in hope, be patient in tribulation, be constant in prayer. [13] Contribute to the needs of the saints and seek to show hospitality.
> [14] Bless those who persecute you; bless and do not curse them. [15] Rejoice with those who rejoice, weep with those who weep. [16] Live in harmony with one another. Do not be haughty, but associate with the lowly.[b] Never be wise in your own sight. [17] Repay no one evil for evil, but give thought to do what is honorable in the sight of all. [18] If possible, so far as it depends on you, live peaceably with all. [19] Beloved, never avenge yourselves, but leave it[c] to the wrath of God, for it is written, "Vengeance is mine, I will repay, says the

LESSON 1:
WHAT IS UN-FORGIVENESS? WHAT CONTRIBUTES TO IT?

> Lord." 20 To the contrary, "if your enemy is hungry, feed him; if he is thirsty, give him something to drink; for by so doing you will heap burning coals on his head." 21 Do not be overcome by evil, but overcome evil with good.

(Romans 12:9-21)—we return to minimal. Why?

_____
_____
_____
_____
_____

If we are walking in selfishness, it stays at partial or complete. Why?

_____
_____
_____
_____
_____

Because of:
- Self-will
- Self-centered
- Self-agenda

> **Read Romans 1:18-25.**
>
> God's Wrath on Unrighteousness
> 18 For the wrath of God is revealed from heaven against all ungodliness and unrighteousness of men, who by their unrighteousness suppress the truth. 19 For what can be known about God is plain to them, because God has shown it to them. 20 For his invisible attributes, namely, his eternal power and divine nature, have been clearly perceived, ever since the creation of the world,[a] in the things that have been made. So they are without excuse. 21 For although they knew God, they did not honor him as God or give thanks to

LESSON 1:
WHAT IS UN-FORGIVENESS? WHAT CONTRIBUTES TO IT?

> him, but they became futile in their thinking, and their foolish hearts were darkened. [22] Claiming to be wise, they became fools, [23] and exchanged the glory of the immortal God for images resembling mortal man and birds and animals and creeping things.
>
> [24] Therefore God gave them up in the lusts of their hearts to impurity, to the dishonoring of their bodies among themselves, [25] because they exchanged the truth about God for a lie and worshiped and served the creature rather than the Creator, who is blessed forever! Amen.

How will an unbeliever operating without the Spirit of God normally respond?

_____
_____
_____
_____
_____

> **Read Romans 8:5-8.**
>
> [5] For those who live according to the flesh set their minds on the things of the flesh, but those who live according to the Spirit set their minds on the things of the Spirit. [6] For to set the mind on the flesh is death, but to set the mind on the Spirit is life and peace. [7] For the mind that is set on the flesh is hostile to God, for it does not submit to God's law; indeed, it cannot. [8] Those who are in the flesh cannot please God.

How will a believer, operating carnally, in the flesh, respond?

_____
_____
_____
_____
_____

LESSON 1:
WHAT IS UN-FORGIVENESS? WHAT CONTRIBUTES TO IT?

Read James 3:14-16.

[14] But if you have bitter jealousy and selfish ambition in your hearts, do not boast and be false to the truth. [15] This is not the wisdom that comes down from above, but is earthly, unspiritual, demonic. [16] For where jealousy and selfish ambition exist, there will be disorder and every vile practice. [17] But the wisdom from above is first pure, then peaceable, gentle, open to reason, full of mercy and good fruits, impartial and sincere. [18] And a harvest of righteousness is sown in peace by those who make peace.

In situations where two or more selfish people are involved in an occurrence of hurt or dispute, these selfish people promote un-forgiveness that deepens the level of response in both. Why?

_____
_____
_____
_____
_____

Read James 4:1-6; 4:11-12.

Warning Against Worldliness

4 What causes quarrels and what causes fights among you? Is it not this, that your passions[a] are at war within you?[b] [2] You desire and do not have, so you murder. You covet and cannot obtain, so you fight and quarrel. You do not have, because you do not ask. [3] You ask and do not receive, because you ask wrongly, to spend it on your passions. [4] You adulterous people![c] Do you not know that friendship with the world is enmity with God? Therefore whoever wishes to be a friend of the world makes himself an enemy of God. [5] Or do you suppose it is to no purpose that the Scripture says, "He yearns jealously over the spirit that he has made to dwell in us"? [6] But he gives more grace. Therefore it says, "God opposes the proud but gives grace to the humble."

LESSON 1:
WHAT IS UN-FORGIVENESS? WHAT CONTRIBUTES TO IT?

> [11] Do not speak evil against one another, brothers.[a] The one who speaks against a brother or judges his brother, speaks evil against the law and judges the law. But if you judge the law, you are not a doer of the law but a judge. [12] There is only one lawgiver and judge, he who is able to save and to destroy. But who are you to judge your neighbor?

The selfish position of each asserts:

- I want…
- I really do not care about what you want…
- I am going to do…

Within this selfishness, there are underlying contributors to un-forgiveness that tend to deepen the level at which we operate:
Normal:

- Difference in personality.

Abnormal:

- Continuing unmet expectations
- Guilt
- Purposeful hurt
- Lack of follow through
- Wounds

- **Continuing unmet expectations**

- **Guilt**

- **Wounds**

LESSON 1:
WHAT IS UN-FORGIVENESS? WHAT CONTRIBUTES TO IT?

- **Other people's interactions with us:**

  - **Purposeful hurt**

  - **Lack of follow through**

Though we have covered the "normal" and "abnormal" factors which contribute to how we respond to wounds, there is yet another: spiritual attack from the enemy.

> **Read Ephesians 6:11-12.**
>
> [11] Put on the whole armor of God, that you may be able to stand against the schemes of the devil. [12] For we do not wrestle against flesh and blood, but against the rulers, against the authorities, against the cosmic powers over this present darkness, against the spiritual forces of evil in the heavenly places.

Where is the enemy working with his schemes and strategies to intensify the anger and the conflict of these situations?

_____
_____
_____
_____
_____
_____

LESSON 1:
WHAT IS UN-FORGIVENESS? WHAT CONTRIBUTES TO IT?

SUMMARY:

What insight have these verses given me regarding where my responses are and the explanation for my responses?

LESSON 1:
WHAT IS UN-FORGIVENESS? WHAT CONTRIBUTES TO IT?

> "A comment or a supposed circumstance can be interpreted in many ways, and if its interpretation causes fear, anxiety, or worry, then it can easily go to anger and frustration."

LESSON 2:
WHY WE WITHHOLD FORGIVENESS

When you take into account everything we've discussed so far and reflect upon the words and meaning, why do we continue to hold on to un-forgiveness? Why is it so difficult to move beyond the hurt and merely forgive? Why do we choose to punish ourselves in retaining our anger and animosity and keep our hearts imprisoned when Christ came to set us free?

> **Read Romans 1:26-32.**
>
> 26 For this reason God gave them up to dishonorable passions. For their women exchanged natural relations for those that are contrary to nature; 27 and the men likewise gave up natural relations with women and were consumed with passion for one another, men committing shameless acts with men and receiving in themselves the due penalty for their error.
>
> 28 And since they did not see fit to acknowledge God, God gave them up to a debased mind to do what ought not to be done. 29 They were filled with all manner of unrighteousness, evil, covetousness, malice. They are full of envy, murder, strife, deceit, maliciousness. They are gossips, 30 slanderers, haters of God, insolent, haughty, boastful, inventors of evil, disobedient to parents, 31 foolish, faithless, heartless, ruthless. 32 Though they know God's righteous decree that those who practice such things deserve to die, they not only do them but give approval to those who practice them.

> "We are so wounded and have been for so long that we have retrained our minds to shy away from any type of constructive criticism."

_____
_____
_____
_____
_____
_____

LESSON 2:
WHY WE WITHHOLD FORGIVENESS

Review some of the reasons we tend to hold on to un-forgiveness:

- Hurts and pain are so deep that they never get to healing.

- I am so poor at handling conflict (rarely get anywhere and tend to be out maneuvered) and find that it is much easier to avoid conflict than deal with it. Over time, this pattern of avoiding conflict becomes my normal way of handling things. I just live with it.

HOW WE CONFUSE FORGIVENESS WITH RECONCILIATION:

The most prevalent reason we withhold forgiveness is: WE CONFUSE FORGIVENESS WITH RECONCILIATION. We think that forgiveness means that I am "reconciling to" or "accepting" fully regarding all that a person has done to hurt or offend me. Unless that person has admitted to what they have done and then apologized, this reconciliation means that I am now accepting what they have done as okay without them having to deal with the injustice of what they have done. So, unless the other party is willing to process through to "real" reconciliation, I can't get to "real" forgiveness. This is a difficult concept, one that we will help clear up in the next few chapters.

Because of this confusion, my thinking is that: If I forgive, I incorrectly believe that:

I will never be able to share my real feelings, hurts, pain, and anger.

I may stimulate further conflict with the other person who may be stronger than me (in personality, in emotion, in hostility, in authority, and power over me—either formally or historically, i.e., with a mother or father, even though I am an adult), and I will just make things worse. It is simply too much trouble.

I will reinforce that what the other person did is okay, and they never have to deal with or have any consequences to what they did. They will only get stronger in their selfishness.

I end up sanctioning and promoting the other person doing this again to me—in fact, over and over again to me.

LESSON 2:
WHY WE WITHHOLD FORGIVENESS

By holding on to my un-forgiveness, I control the dynamics. I make sure these things that I believe do not happen. Actually, by maintaining my coldness and distance in un-forgiveness, I believe that I am:

- Protecting my heart from further hurts and pains.

- Making a statement that what the other person did was wrong, and the other person should feel:

  - Guilt

  - My disapproval

  - Sad at our changed relationship

  - That I no longer will not allow the other person to do this again easily and keep hurting me. This deadens my pain and allows me to scab over my wounds.

  - The consequences of not having me serve you and miss out on the benefits of our past relationship.

  - My need to function by avoiding conflict and by setting up walls around me to protect me.

Actually, what is happening to my heart is quite the opposite (write out the truth of these verses):

> **Read Proverbs 14:10.**
>
> ¹⁰The heart knows its own bitterness, and no stranger shares its joy.

_____
_____
_____
_____
_____

LESSON 2:
WHY WE WITHHOLD FORGIVENESS

> **Read Ephesians 4:30-31.**
>
> ³⁰ And do not grieve the Holy Spirit of God, by whom you were sealed for the day of redemption. ³¹ Let all bitterness and wrath and anger and clamor and slander be put away from you, along with all malice.

_____
_____
_____
_____

> **Read Hebrews 12:15.**
>
> ¹⁵ See to it that no one fails to obtain the grace of God; that no "root of bitterness" springs up and causes trouble, and by it many become defiled.

_____
_____
_____
_____

> **Read Jeremiah 17:5-6; 17:9.**
>
> ⁵ Thus says the Lord:
> "Cursed is the man who trusts in man
>   and makes flesh his strength,[a]
>   whose heart turns away from the Lord.
> ⁶ He is like a shrub in the desert,

LESSON 2:
WHY WE WITHHOLD FORGIVENESS

> and shall not see any good come.
> He shall dwell in the parched places of the wilderness,
>   in an uninhabited salt land.
>
> ⁹ The heart is deceitful above all things,
>   and desperately sick;
>   who can understand it?

_____
_____
_____
_____
_____

There are other wounds and issues in my life that contribute to my inability to go to forgiveness: (Write descriptions of what they are and how they are impacting your life at the moment.)

_____
_____
_____
_____
_____

LESSON 2:
WHY WE WITHHOLD FORGIVENESS

Up to this point, we may have tried to convince ourselves that withholding forgiveness to those who have wounded us actually protects us, but that is a lie. God's Word says that as we continually walk in the flesh and operate in the carnal self, we experience the three consequences listed in Romans 8:5-8: death of the Spirit, enmity against God, and the inability to please God. It's as if we operate as there were no God, and believers operate as practical atheists. Our hearts subsequently move deeper into un-forgiveness, and the emotions we experience or think we control actually cause:

- Deepening of Wounds
- Roots of Bitterness
- Edginess
- Frustration
- Low-grade Anger
- Short Fuses, Triggers, and Hot-buttons
- A feeling of being locked up, in bondage
- Negativity in our energy or outlook; critical feelings

Look at your life and your attitude toward life as a whole. How would you define it? Do you experience joy, peace, and general order? Do you generally live in fear and are critical of others? Does your life reflect the promises of Scripture for those who walk in the Spirit, or does it look quite the opposite? Be honest with yourself, because the fruit of living in the Spirit cannot be falsely generated. If you are not enjoying the abundant life Christ promised to His children, then begin to look at un-forgiveness in your life. Against whom do you hold grudges or hostility? Who are you icy toward or roll your eyes at when they walk into the room? Start with the obvious ones and then allow the Spirit to guide you into further truth as you begin to look at forgiving that high school teacher, the college roommate, your uncle, your boss.

LESSON 2:
WHY WE WITHHOLD FORGIVENESS

Write what you have learned about why you tend to hold on to "un-forgiveness" and where the Lord wants to bring healing and restoration. Journal your thoughts and feelings about these issues and what the Lord is speaking to you about these.

> "Un-forgiveness is literally the root of Christians living in bondage, oppression, and unhappiness instead of the fullness of all Christ promised."

LESSON 2:
WHY WE WITHHOLD FORGIVENESS

LESSON 3:
WHAT IS FORGIVENESS? (PART 1)

> "When you forgive, you are releasing your anger against your offender and have decided to terminate all resentment toward them."

Dictionary definition: Compassionate feelings that allow a person to pardon another: release and conclude resentment, indignation, or anger as a result of a perceived offense, difference, or mistake.

These feelings and ability to pardon another come from God. In fact, it is GOD HIMSELF—His nature! His nature is grace and compassion that releases the wrath and anger that we all deserve because of what we have done, this, as we know, is SIN.

Before we jump right into defining what forgiveness is, I want to give a very practical example from my own life. Do you remember when I was discussing my relationship with my mother? Through that strained relationship God revealed to me what bondage and oppression look like when dealing with unforgiveness. He also reminded me that I had an example from my past of what true forgiveness looks like.

In college, I worked for an advertising company and was responsible for compiling all materials needed for use in client presentations, (remember, these were the days before computers, so all the materials were hard copy). Because I continually demonstrated competence in completing projects, the partners began trusting my ability to correctly execute given assignments. One project, where we all were working toward securing a big client, I received an assignment requiring a very lengthy and complex list of materials to be complied for an important meeting. The presentation package was put together, and I treated it like the rest of my projects at the time and believed it to be correct. The day before the presentation, one of the partners asked me to verify that all of the information was correct. He asked me to get back to him once I had finished checking. I said I would call him back. However, the next day I had a term paper due and needed to stay up late to complete it. Since I assumed the packet was correct, I did not take the extra time to physically doublecheck my work. Yet, I called the partner anyway and told him everything was in order. The next day during the presentation, the final three slides, the "punchline" of the entire meeting, were missing. Not only were the partners not able to illustrate their creative approach to their client, they also presented themselves as an agency that could not pay attention to details. Needless to say, my company lost

LESSON 3:
WHAT IS FORGIVENESS? (PART 1)

that account, and the fault rested squarely upon my shoulders. I failed to fulfill my assignment on top of lying about verifying my work. I had every right to be fired. Yet, I was shown forgiveness and grace. When one of the partners called me into his office, he discussed how my lack of integrity affected him, his business integrity, as well as the integrity of the agency. Then he said he was giving me a gift in keeping my job, that he believed I would learn a valuable life lesson as a result of this mistake. He encouraged me to leave my mistake behind me and only look forward to becoming the best I could be. Instead of firing me, he gave me even more responsibility! What an amazing example of forgiveness, a wonderful demonstration of what forgiveness really looks like.

In light of this story from my past, I ask you: What exactly is forgiveness? What are the true dimensions of forgiveness? What does it feel like? We can start to explain forgiveness by saying it includes having compassionate feelings toward a person who wronged you, and these feelings allow you to pardon them. But forgiveness is more than mere feelings. When you forgive, you are releasing your anger against your offender and have decided to terminate all resentment toward them. So, all of that indignation and anger that bubbled up as the result of difference of opinions or a simple mistake or offense no longer are held against your wrongdoer. You decide to let it go; you choose not to hold on to the offense any longer. Remember the agency partner? He addressed my mistakes, reminded me that those mistakes were worthy of causing termination, and told me to learn from them. Not only that, but he chose not to hold those against me and encouraged me to not hold them against myself, to move on, and simply use my mistakes as a springboard for becoming even better. Those feelings of compassion that allowed him to forgive me and that allow you to likewise forgive others, come from God Himself. In fact, God's very nature is the compassion and grace He freely bestows upon us. We are the ones who deserve the wrath and anger of God because of the sin we have committed, but God releases that wrath and no longer holds it against us. God forgives us and, simply, lets our sin go.

What are the elements of forgiveness as defined by these verses?

> **Read Psalm 130:3-4; 130:7.**
>
> [3] If you, O Lord, should mark iniquities,
>   O Lord, who could stand?
> [4] But with you there is forgiveness,
>   that you may be feared.

LESSON 3:
WHAT IS FORGIVENESS? (PART 1)

> ⁷ O Israel, hope in the Lord!
> For with the Lord there is steadfast love,
> and with him is plentiful redemption.

_____
_____
_____
_____

Read Psalm 103:8-12.

> ⁸ The Lord is merciful and gracious,
> slow to anger and abounding in steadfast love.
> ⁹ He will not always chide,
> nor will he keep his anger forever.
> ¹⁰ He does not deal with us according to our sins,
> nor repay us according to our iniquities.
> ¹¹ For as high as the heavens are above the earth,
> so great is his steadfast love toward those who fear him;
> ¹² as far as the east is from the west,
> so far does he remove our transgressions from us.

_____
_____
_____
_____

LESSON 3:
WHAT IS FORGIVENESS? (PART 1)

> **God is eternally holy—perfectly righteous. Read Isaiah 6:3.**
>
> 3 And one called to another and said:
> "Holy, holy, holy is the Lord of hosts;
> the whole earth is full of his glory!"[a]

> **Read Revelation 4:8-11.**
>
> 8 And the four living creatures, each of them with six wings, are full of eyes all around and within, and day and night they never cease to say,
> "Holy, holy, holy, is the Lord God Almighty,
>   who was and is and is to come!"
> 9 And whenever the living creatures give glory and honor and thanks to him who is seated on the throne, who lives forever and ever, 10 the twenty-four elders fall down before him who is seated on the throne and worship him who lives forever and ever. They cast their crowns before the throne, saying,
> 11 "Worthy are you, our Lord and God,
>   to receive glory and honor and power,
> for you created all things,
>   and by your will they existed and were created."

LESSON 3:
WHAT IS FORGIVENESS? (PART 1)

When Scripture speaks of holiness, it means something or someone is wholly distinct, separate, in a class all by themselves. R. C. Sproul explains it this way in his book, *The Holiness of God*:

> The primary meaning of holy is "separate." It comes from an ancient word that meant, "to cut," or "to separate." Perhaps even more accurate would be the phrase "a cut above something." When we find a garment or another piece of merchandise that is outstanding, that has a superior excellence, we use the expression that it is "a cut above the rest."

So, God is unique and has no rivals or competition. He is completely other than anyone or anything else in all creation. But God's holiness encompasses so much more. God's holiness also means He is worthy of all honor and power and glory (praise, fame, and/or adoration). If God is worth such accolades, which we call worship, He must also be pure, having no wrong or evil in Him—which is true! God is good, He is morally pure, He loves perfectly and is perfect love, and every action He does is the same. God is the only perfect being, and since He is perfectly righteous (morally upright and above reproach) to forgive others as He has forgiven us certainly is divine.

Take a minute to let all these wonderful truths sink into your head and heart. The last thing you need to do is to rush past the truths contained within these Scriptures. Ask yourself, what does it mean to me that God's very nature is to forgive? How does this one statement change your perception of God and your relationship with Him? When you begin to grasp this reality, it makes more sense to also embrace how God is truly other, wholly different than the humanity He created. Only the One who is wholly different, who is holy, can have a nature defined by forgiveness. This forgiveness, spurred on by His never ending love toward His children, is waiting for you to receive it. Spend ample time letting these statements become truth to you, become life for you, and thank the Father for His nature.

God's Original Plan

This holy and wholly other and different God delighted in creating, and still does! So, when God created Adam and Eve in the garden, He created them perfectly. They were holy as He is holy, perfect, and righteous. He created them to have an exceptional life and constant communion with Himself. God created man to have a full and enjoyable relationship with their Creator.

LESSON 3:
WHAT IS FORGIVENESS? (PART 1)

As you read through this section of Scripture that speaks to God's original plan for our lives, write down the exceptional characteristics of this life:

Read Genesis 1:26-2:25.

26 Then God said, "Let us make man[a] in our image, after our likeness. And let them have dominion over the fish of the sea and over the birds of the heavens and over the livestock and over all the earth and over every creeping thing that creeps on the earth."

27 So God created man in his own image,
in the image of God he created him;
male and female he created them.

28 And God blessed them. And God said to them, "Be fruitful and multiply and fill the earth and subdue it, and have dominion over the fish of the sea and over the birds of the heavens and over every living thing that moves on the earth." 29 And God said, "Behold, I have given you every plant yielding seed that is on the face of all the earth, and every tree with seed in its fruit. You shall have them for food. 30 And to every beast of the earth and to every bird of the heavens and to everything that creeps on the earth, everything that has the breath of life, I have given every green plant for food." And it was so. 31 And God saw everything that he had made, and behold, it was very good. And there was evening and there was morning, the sixth day.

The Seventh Day, God Rests
2 Thus the heavens and the earth were finished, and all the host of them. 2 And on the seventh day God finished his work that he had done, and he rested on the seventh day from all his work that he had done. 3 So God blessed the seventh day and made it holy, because on it God rested from all his work that he had done in creation.

The Creation of Man and Woman
4 These are the generations
of the heavens and the earth when they were created,
in the day that the Lord God made the earth and the heavens.

5 When no bush of the field[b] was yet in the land[c] and no small plant of the field had yet sprung up—for the Lord God had not caused it to rain on the land, and

LESSON 3:
WHAT IS FORGIVENESS? (PART 1)

there was no man to work the ground, ⁶ and a mist[d] was going up from the land and was watering the whole face of the ground— ⁷ then the Lord God formed the man of dust from the ground and breathed into his nostrils the breath of life, and the man became a living creature. ⁸ And the Lord God planted a garden in Eden, in the east, and there he put the man whom he had formed. ⁹ And out of the ground the Lord God made to spring up every tree that is pleasant to the sight and good for food. The tree of life was in the midst of the garden, and the tree of the knowledge of good and evil.

¹⁰ A river flowed out of Eden to water the garden, and there it divided and became four rivers. ¹¹ The name of the first is the Pishon. It is the one that flowed around the whole land of Havilah, where there is gold. ¹² And the gold of that land is good; bdellium and onyx stone are there. ¹³ The name of the second river is the Gihon. It is the one that flowed around the whole land of Cush. ¹⁴ And the name of the third river is the Tigris, which flows east of Assyria. And the fourth river is the Euphrates.

¹⁵ The Lord God took the man and put him in the garden of Eden to work it and keep it. ¹⁶ And the Lord God commanded the man, saying, "You may surely eat of every tree of the garden, ¹⁷ but of the tree of the knowledge of good and evil you shall not eat, for in the day that you eat[e] of it you shall surely die."
¹⁸ Then the Lord God said, "It is not good that the man should be alone; I will make him a helper fit for[f] him." ¹⁹ Now out of the ground the Lord God had formed[g] every beast of the field and every bird of the heavens and brought them to the man to see what he would call them. And whatever the man called every living creature, that was its name. ²⁰ The man gave names to all livestock and to the birds of the heavens and to every beast of the field. But for Adam[h] there was not found a helper fit for him. ²¹ So the Lord God caused a deep sleep to fall upon the man, and while he slept took one of his ribs and closed up its place with flesh. ²² And the rib that the Lord God had taken from the man he made[i] into a woman and brought her to the man. ²³ Then the man said,

"This at last is bone of my bones
 and flesh of my flesh;
she shall be called Woman,
 because she was taken out of Man."[j]

²⁴ Therefore a man shall leave his father and his mother and hold fast to his wife, and they shall become one flesh. ²⁵ And the man and his wife were both naked and were not ashamed.

LESSON 3:
WHAT IS FORGIVENESS? (PART 1)

_____
_____
_____
_____
_____

The 7 Exceptional characteristics are:

- Exceptional Authority
- Exceptional Provision
- Exceptional Work
- Exceptional Relationships (marriage)
- Exceptional Identity
- Exceptional Health & Healing
- Exceptional Communion with God

Our Failing and Falling

When God created the garden and the first humans in perfection, He told Adam and Eve they could eat of any tree except for the tree of the knowledge of good and evil. Remember, Eden is said to have had four rivers coming together in it. Although the exact size of Eden is unsure, we can assume it was quite expansive. This being said, there was a plethora of fruit-bearing trees for man and woman to eat from, and only one tree to avoid. Even with myriads of choices for food, Adam and Even chose to eat of that tree, against the will of God, and because of their willful act of the flesh, they sinned. This changed everything.

Adam and Eve exercised self-will and disobeyed God—choosing to eat of the tree of the knowledge of good and evil. This was mankind's first SIN (the exercise of self-will against the will of God).

> **Read Genesis 3:1-7.**
>
> The Fall
> **3** Now the serpent was more crafty than any other beast of the field that the Lord God had made.
>
> He said to the woman, "Did God actually say, 'You[a] shall not eat of any tree in the garden'?"2 And the woman said to the serpent, "We may eat of the fruit of the trees in the garden, 3 but God said, 'You shall not eat of the fruit of the tree

LESSON 3:
WHAT IS FORGIVENESS? (PART 1)

> that is in the midst of the garden, neither shall you touch it, lest you die."' 4 But the serpent said to the woman, "You will not surely die. 5 For God knows that when you eat of it your eyes will be opened, and you will be like God, knowing good and evil." 6 So when the woman saw that the tree was good for food, and that it was a delight to the eyes, and that the tree was to be desired to make one wise,[b] she took of its fruit and ate, and she also gave some to her husband who was with her, and he ate. 7 Then the eyes of both were opened, and they knew that they were naked. And they sewed fig leaves together and made themselves loincloths.

Read Genesis 2:16-17.

> 16 And the Lord God commanded the man, saying, "You may surely eat of every tree of the garden, 17 but of the tree of the knowledge of good and evil you shall not eat, for in the day that you eat[a] of it you shall surely die."

What happened with how Adam and Eve surrendered to the appeal of Satan and what were the consequences? - then put blank lines after each set of verses.

Read Genesis 3:7-24.

> 7 Then the eyes of both were opened, and they knew that they were naked. And they sewed fig leaves together and made themselves loincloths.
> 8 And they heard the sound of the Lord God walking in the garden in the cool[a] of the day, and the man and his wife hid themselves from the presence of the Lord God among the trees of the garden. 9 But the Lord God called to the man and said to him, "Where are you?"[b] 10 And he said, "I heard the sound of you in the garden, and I was afraid, because I was naked, and I hid myself." 11 He said, "Who told you that you were naked? Have you eaten of the tree of which I commanded you not to eat?" 12 The man said, "The woman whom you gave to be with me, she gave me fruit of the tree, and I ate." 13 Then the Lord God said to the woman, "What

LESSON 3:
WHAT IS FORGIVENESS? (PART 1)

is this that you have done?" The woman said, "The serpent deceived me, and I ate."

14 The Lord God said to the serpent,

"Because you have done this,
    cursed are you above all livestock
    and above all beasts of the field;
on your belly you shall go,
    and dust you shall eat
    all the days of your life.
15 I will put enmity between you and the woman,
    and between your offspring[c] and her offspring;
he shall bruise your head,
    and you shall bruise his heel."

16 To the woman he said,

"I will surely multiply your pain in childbearing;
    in pain you shall bring forth children.
Your desire shall be contrary to[d] your husband,
    but he shall rule over you."

17 And to Adam he said,

"Because you have listened to the voice of your wife
    and have eaten of the tree
of which I commanded you,
    'You shall not eat of it,'
cursed is the ground because of you;
    in pain you shall eat of it all the days of your life;
18 thorns and thistles it shall bring forth for you;
    and you shall eat the plants of the field.
19 By the sweat of your face
    you shall eat bread,
till you return to the ground,
    for out of it you were taken;
for you are dust,
    and to dust you shall return."

20 The man called his wife's name Eve, because she was the mother of all living. [e] 21 And the Lord God made for Adam and for his wife garments of skins and clothed them.

LESSON 3:
WHAT IS FORGIVENESS? (PART 1)

> ²² Then the Lord God said, "Behold, the man has become like one of us in knowing good and evil. Now, lest he reach out his hand and take also of the tree of life and eat, and live forever—" ²³ therefore the Lord God sent him out from the garden of Eden to work the ground from which he was taken. ²⁴ He drove out the man, and at the east of the garden of Eden he placed the cherubim and a flaming sword that turned every way to guard the way to the tree of life.

At this point, man and woman deserved God's eternal wrath and anger. His holy creation wronged the Holy Creator. What were the consequences of this?

> **Read Psalm 103:9-10.**
>
> ⁹ He will not always chide,
>   nor will he keep his anger forever.
> ¹⁰ He does not deal with us according to our sins,
>   nor repay us according to our iniquities.

_____
_____
_____
_____

> **Read Psalm 143:2.**
>
> ² Enter not into judgment with your servant,
>   for no one living is righteous before you.

_____
_____
_____
_____

LESSON 3:
WHAT IS FORGIVENESS? (PART 1)

> **Read Psalm 130:3.**
>
> ³ If you, O Lord, should mark iniquities,
>   O Lord, who could stand?

_____
_____
_____
_____
_____

Why do we deserve God's eternal wrath, and why (unless He offered an opportunity for forgiveness through His nature) would we would live eternally separated from Him? Think through the implication of this regarding our process of forgiveness and write your answers here.

_____
_____
_____
_____
_____
_____
_____
_____
_____
_____
_____
_____
_____

LESSON 4:
WHAT IS FORGIVENESS? (PART 2)

Review your notes from Lesson 3, and restate the reason we deserve God's eternal wrath.

In the Old Testament, God's forgiveness was fulfilled through the sacrifice of a perfect lamb, once a year by the high priest on the Day of Atonement. It was the shedding of innocent blood in an exchange of the lamb's life for the lives of the people of Israel.

> **Read Leviticus 16-17 noting both the reasons we have access to God's forgiveness and the instructions for how Israel received atonement (forgiveness) for their iniquity once a year.**
>
> The Day of Atonement
> **16** The Lord spoke to Moses after the death of the two sons of Aaron, when they drew near before the Lord and died, ² and the Lord said to Moses, "Tell Aaron your brother not to come at any time into the Holy Place inside the veil, before the mercy seat that is on the ark, so that he may not die. For I will appear in the cloud over the mercy seat. ³ But in this way Aaron shall come into the Holy Place: with a bull from the herd for a sin offering and a ram for a burnt offering. ⁴ He shall put on the holy linen coat and shall have the linen undergarment on his body, and he shall tie the linen sash around his waist, and wear the linen turban; these are the holy garments. He shall bathe his body in water and then put them on. ⁵ And he shall take from the congregation of the people of Israel two male goats for a sin offering, and one ram for a burnt offering.
>
> ⁶ "Aaron shall offer the bull as a sin offering for himself and shall make atonement for himself and for his house. ⁷ Then he shall take the two goats and set them before the Lord at the entrance of the tent of meeting. ⁸ And Aaron shall cast lots over the two goats, one lot for the Lord and the other lot for Azazel.[a] ⁹ And Aaron shall present the goat on which the lot fell for the Lord and use it as a sin offering, ¹⁰ but the goat

> "In the New Testament, God's forgiveness was fulfilled through the sacrifice (the exchange of Christ's life for our life) of The Perfect Lamb of God (the Father's only begotten Son, and our High Priest). It was once and for all, completed, finished."

LESSON 4:
WHAT IS FORGIVENESS? (PART 2)

on which the lot fell for Azazel shall be presented alive before the Lord to make atonement over it, that it may be sent away into the wilderness to Azazel.

[11] "Aaron shall present the bull as a sin offering for himself, and shall make atonement for himself and for his house. He shall kill the bull as a sin offering for himself. [12] And he shall take a censer full of coals of fire from the altar before the Lord, and two handfuls of sweet incense beaten small, and he shall bring it inside the veil [13] and put the incense on the fire before the Lord, that the cloud of the incense may cover the mercy seat that is over the testimony, so that he does not die. [14] And he shall take some of the blood of the bull and sprinkle it with his finger on the front of the mercy seat on the east side, and in front of the mercy seat he shall sprinkle some of the blood with his finger seven times.

[15] "Then he shall kill the goat of the sin offering that is for the people and bring its blood inside the veil and do with its blood as he did with the blood of the bull, sprinkling it over the mercy seat and in front of the mercy seat. [16] Thus he shall make atonement for the Holy Place, because of the uncleannesses of the people of Israel and because of their transgressions, all their sins. And so he shall do for the tent of meeting, which dwells with them in the midst of their uncleannesses. [17] No one may be in the tent of meeting from the time he enters to make atonement in the Holy Place until he comes out and has made atonement for himself and for his house and for all the assembly of Israel. [18] Then he shall go out to the altar that is before the Lord and make atonement for it, and shall take some of the blood of the bull and some of the blood of the goat, and put it on the horns of the altar all around. [19] And he shall sprinkle some of the blood on it with his finger seven times, and cleanse it and consecrate it from the uncleannesses of the people of Israel.

[20] "And when he has made an end of atoning for the Holy Place and the tent of meeting and the altar, he shall present the live goat. [21] And Aaron shall lay both his hands on the head of the live goat, and confess over it all the iniquities of the people of Israel, and all their transgressions, all their sins. And he shall put them on the head of the goat and send it away into the wilderness by the hand of a man who is in readiness. [22] The goat shall bear all their iniquities on itself to a remote area, and he shall let the goat go free in the wilderness.

LESSON 4:
WHAT IS FORGIVENESS? (PART 2)

23 "Then Aaron shall come into the tent of meeting and shall take off the linen garments that he put on when he went into the Holy Place and shall leave them there. 24 And he shall bathe his body in water in a holy place and put on his garments and come out and offer his burnt offering and the burnt offering of the people and make atonement for himself and for the people. 25 And the fat of the sin offering he shall burn on the altar. 26 And he who lets the goat go to Azazel shall wash his clothes and bathe his body in water, and afterward he may come into the camp. 27 And the bull for the sin offering and the goat for the sin offering, whose blood was brought in to make atonement in the Holy Place, shall be carried outside the camp. Their skin and their flesh and their dung shall be burned up with fire. 28 And he who burns them shall wash his clothes and bathe his body in water, and afterward he may come into the camp.

29 "And it shall be a statute to you forever that in the seventh month, on the tenth day of the month, you shall afflict yourselves[b] and shall do no work, either the native or the stranger who sojourns among you. 30 For on this day shall atonement be made for you to cleanse you. You shall be clean before the Lord from all your sins. 31 It is a Sabbath of solemn rest to you, and you shall afflict yourselves; it is a statute forever. 32 And the priest who is anointed and consecrated as priest in his father's place shall make atonement, wearing the holy linen garments. 33 He shall make atonement for the holy sanctuary, and he shall make atonement for the tent of meeting and for the altar, and he shall make atonement for the priests and for all the people of the assembly. 34 And this shall be a statute forever for you, that atonement may be made for the people of Israel once in the year because of all their sins." And Aaron[c] did as the Lord commanded Moses.

The Place of Sacrifice
17 And the Lord spoke to Moses, saying, 2 "Speak to Aaron and his sons and to all the people of Israel and say to them, this is the thing that the Lord has commanded. 3 If any one of the house of Israel kills an ox or a lamb or a goat in the camp, or kills it outside the camp,4 and does not bring it to the entrance of the tent of meeting to offer it as a gift to the Lord in front of the tabernacle of the Lord, bloodguilt shall be imputed to that man. He has shed blood, and that man shall be cut off from among his people. 5 This is to the end that the people of Israel may bring their sacrifices that they sacrifice in the open field, that they may bring them to the Lord, to the priest at the entrance of the tent of meeting, and sacrifice them as sacrifices of peace offerings to the Lord. 6 And the priest

LESSON 4:
WHAT IS FORGIVENESS? (PART 2)

shall throw the blood on the altar of the Lord at the entrance of the tent of meeting and burn the fat for a pleasing aroma to the Lord. 7 So they shall no more sacrifice their sacrifices to goat demons, after whom they whore. This shall be a statute forever for them throughout their generations.

8 "And you shall say to them, any one of the house of Israel, or of the strangers who sojourn among them, who offers a burnt offering or sacrifice 9 and does not bring it to the entrance of the tent of meeting to offer it to the Lord, that man shall be cut off from his people.

Laws Against Eating Blood
10 "If any one of the house of Israel or of the strangers who sojourn among them eats any blood, I will set my face against that person who eats blood and will cut him off from among his people. 11 For the life of the flesh is in the blood, and I have given it for you on the altar to make atonement for your souls, for it is the blood that makes atonement by the life. 12 Therefore I have said to the people of Israel, no person among you shall eat blood, neither shall any stranger who sojourns among you eat blood.

13 "Any one also of the people of Israel, or of the strangers who sojourn among them, who takes in hunting any beast or bird that may be eaten shall pour out its blood and cover it with earth. 14 For the life of every creature[d] is its blood: its blood is its life.[e] Therefore I have said to the people of Israel, You shall not eat the blood of any creature, for the life of every creature is its blood. Whoever eats it shall be cut off. 15 And every person who eats what dies of itself or what is torn by beasts, whether he is a native or a sojourner, shall wash his clothes and bathe himself in water and be unclean until the evening; then he shall be clean. 16 But if he does not wash them or bathe his flesh, he shall bear his iniquity."

_____
_____
_____
_____
_____

LESSON 4:
WHAT IS FORGIVENESS? (PART 2)

In the New Testament, God's forgiveness was fulfilled through the sacrifice (the exchange of Christ's life for our life) of The Perfect Lamb of God (the Father's only begotten Son, and our High Priest). It was once and for all, completed, finished. It was forgiveness fulfilled for all, for all time. **Read through these verses and identify what Christ has done/completed on our behalf to "forgive" us?**

> **Read Romans 3:21-26.**
>
> The Righteousness of God Through Faith
> 21 But now the righteousness of God has been manifested apart from the law, although the Law and the Prophets bear witness to it— 22 the righteousness of God through faith in Jesus Christ for all who believe. For there is no distinction: 23 for all have sinned and fall short of the glory of God, 24 and are justified by his grace as a gift, through the redemption that is in Christ Jesus, 25 whom God put forward as a propitiation by his blood, to be received by faith. This was to show God's righteousness, because in his divine forbearance he had passed over former sins. 26 It was to show his righteousness at the present time, so that he might be just and the justifier of the one who has faith in Jesus.

_____
_____
_____
_____
_____

> **Read Ephesians 1:7-12.**
>
> 7 In him we have redemption through his blood, the forgiveness of our trespasses, according to the riches of his grace, 8 which he lavished upon us, in all wisdom and insight 9 making known[a] to us the mystery of his will, according to his purpose, which he set forth in Christ 10 as a plan for the fullness of time, to unite all things in him, things in heaven and things on earth.

LESSON 4:
WHAT IS FORGIVENESS? (PART 2)

> ¹¹ In him we have obtained an inheritance, having been predestined according to the purpose of him who works all things according to the counsel of his will, ¹² so that we who were the first to hope in Christ might be to the praise of his glory.

_____
_____
_____
_____
_____

> **Read Hebrews 9:1-10:18.**
>
> The Earthly Holy Place
> **9** Now even the first covenant had regulations for worship and an earthly place of holiness.² For a tent[a] was prepared, the first section, in which were the lampstand and the table and the bread of the Presence.[b] It is called the Holy Place. ³ Behind the second curtain was a second section[c] called the Most Holy Place, ⁴ having the golden altar of incense and the ark of the covenant covered on all sides with gold, in which was a golden urn holding the manna, and Aaron's staff that budded, and the tablets of the covenant. ⁵ Above it were the cherubim of glory overshadowing the mercy seat. Of these things we cannot now speak in detail.
>
> ⁶ These preparations having thus been made, the priests go regularly into the first section, performing their ritual duties, ⁷ but into the second only the high priest goes, and he but once a year, and not without taking blood, which he offers for himself and for the unintentional sins of the people. ⁸ By this the Holy Spirit indicates that the way into the holy places is not yet opened as long as the first section is still standing ⁹ (which is symbolic for the present age).[d] According to this arrangement, gifts and sacrifices are offered that cannot perfect the conscience of the worshiper, ¹⁰ but deal only with food and drink and various washings, regulations for the body imposed until the time of reformation.

LESSON 4:
WHAT IS FORGIVENESS? (PART 2)

Redemption Through the Blood of Christ

[11] But when Christ appeared as a high priest of the good things that have come,[e] then through the greater and more perfect tent (not made with hands, that is, not of this creation) [12] he entered once for all into the holy places, not by means of the blood of goats and calves but by means of his own blood, thus securing an eternal redemption. [13] For if the blood of goats and bulls, and the sprinkling of defiled persons with the ashes of a heifer, sanctify[f] for the purification of the flesh, [14] how much more will the blood of Christ, who through the eternal Spirit offered himself without blemish to God, purify our[g] conscience from dead works to serve the living God.

[15] Therefore he is the mediator of a new covenant, so that those who are called may receive the promised eternal inheritance, since a death has occurred that redeems them from the transgressions committed under the first covenant. [h] [16] For where a will is involved, the death of the one who made it must be established. [17] For a will takes effect only at death, since it is not in force as long as the one who made it is alive. [18] Therefore not even the first covenant was inaugurated without blood. [19] For when every commandment of the law had been declared by Moses to all the people, he took the blood of calves and goats, with water and scarlet wool and hyssop, and sprinkled both the book itself and all the people, [20] saying, "This is the blood of the covenant that God commanded for you." [21] And in the same way he sprinkled with the blood both the tent and all the vessels used in worship. [22] Indeed, under the law almost everything is purified with blood, and without the shedding of blood there is no forgiveness of sins.

[23] Thus it was necessary for the copies of the heavenly things to be purified with these rites, but the heavenly things themselves with better sacrifices than these. [24] For Christ has entered, not into holy places made with hands, which are copies of the true things, but into heaven itself, now to appear in the presence of God on our behalf. [25] Nor was it to offer himself repeatedly, as the high priest enters the holy places every year with blood not his own, [26] for then he would have had to suffer repeatedly since the foundation of the world. But as it is, he has appeared once for all at the end of the ages to put away sin by the sacrifice of himself. [27] And just as it is appointed for man to die once, and after that comes judgment, [28] so Christ, having been offered once to bear the sins of many, will appear a second time, not to deal with sin but to save those who are eagerly waiting for him.

LESSON 4:
WHAT IS FORGIVENESS? (PART 2)

Christ's Sacrifice Once for All

10 For since the law has but a shadow of the good things to come instead of the true form of these realities, it can never, by the same sacrifices that are continually offered every year, make perfect those who draw near. ² Otherwise, would they not have ceased to be offered, since the worshipers, having once been cleansed, would no longer have any consciousness of sins? ³ But in these sacrifices there is a reminder of sins every year. ⁴ For it is impossible for the blood of bulls and goats to take away sins.

⁵ Consequently, when Christ[i] came into the world, he said,

"Sacrifices and offerings you have not desired,
    but a body have you prepared for me;
⁶ in burnt offerings and sin offerings
    you have taken no pleasure.
⁷ Then I said, 'Behold, I have come to do your will, O God,
    as it is written of me in the scroll of the book.'"

⁸ When he said above, "You have neither desired nor taken pleasure in sacrifices and offerings and burnt offerings and sin offerings" (these are offered according to the law), ⁹ then he added, "Behold, I have come to do your will." He does away with the first in order to establish the second. ¹⁰ And by that will we have been sanctified through the offering of the body of Jesus Christ once for all.

¹¹ And every priest stands daily at his service, offering repeatedly the same sacrifices, which can never take away sins. ¹² But when Christ[j] had offered for all time a single sacrifice for sins, he sat down at the right hand of God, ¹³ waiting from that time until his enemies should be made a footstool for his feet. ¹⁴ For by a single offering he has perfected for all time those who are being sanctified.
¹⁵ And the Holy Spirit also bears witness to us; for after saying,
¹⁶ "This is the covenant that I will make with them
    after those days, declares the Lord:
I will put my laws on their hearts,
    and write them on their minds,"
¹⁷ then he adds,
"I will remember their sins and their lawless deeds no more."
¹⁸ Where there is forgiveness of these, there is no longer any offering for sin.

LESSON 4:
WHAT IS FORGIVENESS? (PART 2)

_____
_____
_____
_____
_____

> **Read 1 John 4:7-11.**
>
> God Is Love
> ⁷ Beloved, let us love one another, for love is from God, and whoever loves has been born of God and knows God. ⁸ Anyone who does not love does not know God, because God is love. ⁹ In this the love of God was made manifest among us, that God sent his only Son into the world, so that we might live through him. ¹⁰ In this is love, not that we have loved God but that he loved us and sent his Son to be the propitiation for our sins. ¹¹ Beloved, if God so loved us, we also ought to love one another.

_____
_____
_____
_____
_____

Upon His satisfying the requirements of taking upon Himself the judgment for sin through His death on the cross, He was resurrected into the new, superabundant life eternal. Read through these verses and identify what His resurrection then has provided to us:

LESSON 4:
WHAT IS FORGIVENESS? (PART 2)

Read John 11:17-27.

I Am the Resurrection and the Life

17 Now when Jesus came, he found that Lazarus had already been in the tomb four days. 18 Bethany was near Jerusalem, about two miles[a] off, 19 and many of the Jews had come to Martha and Mary to console them concerning their brother. 20 So when Martha heard that Jesus was coming, she went and met him, but Mary remained seated in the house. 21 Martha said to Jesus, "Lord, if you had been here, my brother would not have died. 22 But even now I know that whatever you ask from God, God will give you." 23 Jesus said to her, "Your brother will rise again." 24 Martha said to him, "I know that he will rise again in the resurrection on the last day." 25 Jesus said to her, "I am the resurrection and the life.[b] Whoever believes in me, though he die, yet shall he live, 26 and everyone who lives and believes in me shall never die. Do you believe this?" 27 She said to him, "Yes, Lord; I believe that you are the Christ, the Son of God, who is coming into the world."

_____
_____
_____
_____
_____

Read John 14:15-26.

Jesus Promises the Holy Spirit

15 "If you love me, you will keep my commandments. 16 And I will ask the Father, and he will give you another Helper,[a] to be with you forever, 17 even the Spirit of truth, whom the world cannot receive, because it neither sees him nor knows him. You know him, for he dwells with you and will be[b] in you.

18 "I will not leave you as orphans; I will come to you. 19 Yet a little while and the world will see me no more, but you will see me. Because I live, you also will live. 20 In that day you will know that I am in my Father, and you in me, and I in you. 21 Whoever has my commandments and keeps them, he it is who

LESSON 4:
WHAT IS FORGIVENESS? (PART 2)

loves me. And he who loves me will be loved by my Father, and I will love him and manifest myself to him." [22] Judas (not Iscariot) said to him, "Lord, how is it that you will manifest yourself to us, and not to the world?" [23] Jesus answered him, "If anyone loves me, he will keep my word, and my Father will love him, and we will come to him and make our home with him. [24] Whoever does not love me does not keep my words. And the word that you hear is not mine but the Father's who sent me.

[25] "These things I have spoken to you while I am still with you. [26] But the Helper, the Holy Spirit, whom the Father will send in my name, he will teach you all things and bring to your remembrance all that I have said to you.

_____

_____

_____

_____

_____

Read John 10:10.

[10] The thief comes only to steal and kill and destroy. I came that they may have life and have it abundantly.

_____

_____

_____

_____

_____

LESSON 4:
WHAT IS FORGIVENESS? (PART 2)

So, in other words:

If His level of forgiveness were based upon what we deserve, then what would happen to us eternally?

_____
_____
_____
_____
_____

(eternal un-forgiveness and separation)

If His level of forgiveness were based upon us doing better and trying harder (good works), then what would happen to us eternally?

_____
_____
_____
_____
_____

(eternal un-forgiveness and separation)

If His level of forgiveness were based upon us asking for a reprieve from a kind and generous judge, then what would happen to us?

_____
_____
_____
_____
_____

(eternal un-forgiveness and separation).

LESSON 4:
WHAT IS FORGIVENESS? (PART 2)

IT IS NOT BASED UPON OUR RESPONSE, BUT UPON HIS NATURE. HE IS FORGIVENESS! AND WITHOUT THIS FORGIVENESS, THERE IS NO POSSIBILITY OF RECONCILIATION.

So, through His death and now living in the Resurrection, has Christ forgiven everyone? _____ *(Yes! Once and for all, it is completed, finished.)*

Does He have any difficulty or struggle in extending forgiveness to anyone? _____*(No! It is already done, completed, finished.)*

Does someone have to fix all their mistakes and act perfectly? _____ *(No)*

Does someone have to live out a "second class," mediocre life and only experience partial forgiveness by:

Staying in guilt? Grief? _____ *(No)*

Being unable to correct things? _____ *(No)*

Being reminded of failures? _____ *(No)*

An inability to regain the best? _____ *(No)*

Does someone have to wait until they perform? _____ *(No)*

How fast can we experience God's forgiveness toward us?

Read 1 John 1:9.

⁹ If we confess our sins, he is faithful and just to forgive us our sins and to cleanse us from all unrighteousness.

LESSON 4:
WHAT IS FORGIVENESS? (PART 2)

_____
_____
_____
_____
_____

(Instantaneous; nanosecond)

Why?

_____
_____
_____
_____
_____

(Not based upon what we do, but on His nature and what He has already done!)

To break things down:

- If God forgave based upon what we deserve, then eternal un-forgiveness and separation would necessarily ensue.

- If God's forgiveness were dependent upon us doing better, trying harder, attempting good works, then eternal un-forgiveness and separation would be inevitable.

- If God based His forgiveness upon us asking for a pardon as from a kind and generous judge, then eternal un-forgiveness and separation would be the sentence.

Be further encouraged by stories from Scripture. God's Word gives us example after example of those who deserved God's wrath, but instead experienced God's forgiveness:

- Noah was known as a drunk, but God used him mightily.

- Abraham lied about who his wife really was, but God gave him the covenant.

LESSON 4:
WHAT IS FORGIVENESS? (PART 2)

- Isaac lied and stole his brother's inheritance, but God changed his name to Israel.

- Moses disobeyed God and had a speech impediment, but he led the Israelites out of Egypt.

- David did his share of sinning but was still known as a man after God's own heart.

- Peter denied Jesus and had a temper but led thousands to the Lord.

- Paul originally killed Christians, but God used him mightily to reach the Gentiles.

> "God's forgiveness is full and complete. There are no 'second class citizens' in the Kingdom."

Write out what you understand as to why God has forgiven us and the key truths about this forgiveness. What do these mean for you personally and your ability to forgive others?

_____
_____
_____
_____
_____
_____
_____
_____
_____
_____
_____
_____
_____
_____
_____
_____

LESSON 4:
WHAT IS FORGIVENESS? (PART 2)

LESSON 5:
WHAT IS RECONCILIATION? (PART 1)

Since God is forgiveness, since it is His nature, and He has finished the work of forgiveness toward us who deserve His wrath and un-forgiveness, the key question is this: Do all people automatically experience this forgiveness? No.

God is forgiving; forgiveness is at the core of His nature. The work done on the cross, once and for all, was and is still very powerful. That work alone is what gives separated and estranged humanity hope of a relationship with a holy and wholly separate and unique God. But even though God has already forgiven all of humanity because of the cross and has no hesitation about to whom He offers it, such forgiveness does not automatically translate into reconciliation. Why doesn't all of humanity experience God's forgiveness? Because forgiveness can only be experienced through true reconciliation. Think about it. When there is a conflict between two people or groups of people, forgiveness is offered by one side because their desire is to once more have a relationship with the other. Each side must process through the offense and hurt done to get to point where each is able to move on, to let go of their anger and frustration. Both parties' expectations for continuing in relationship must be satisfied. Such actions and resolved tension lead to a deeper relationship, a deeper trust, and respect is experienced. Without forgiveness, a relationship cannot exist. Without trust, no relationship can stand.

> "God is forgiving; forgiveness is at the core of His nature. The work done on the cross, once and for all, was and is still very powerful."

Consider this:
Do you experience this forgiveness automatically because of His nature, and thus all experience it? _____ *(No)*

Remember, forgiveness is only experienced by reconciliation. By definition, reconciliation is between two parties. How?

_____
_____
_____
_____
_____

(Each party must process truth to a resolution satisfactory to both parties.)

LESSON 5:
WHAT IS RECONCILIATION? (PART 1)

What is the truth that satisfies Christ's offer of forgiveness to be reconciled to Him?

- God is holy and requires holiness and perfect righteousness.

- He cannot touch nor associate with un-holiness and un-righteousness.

- All have fallen short of this requirement and thus deserve His wrath and eternal separation. We stand condemned.

- He has performed the necessary exchange of His life through His death for our life—satisfying the requirement of holiness and perfect righteousness.

- If we believe this in our heart (soul) to be true, we pass from condemnation to life—reconciled; if we do not believe, we remain condemned, separated from God—not reconciled.

Read these verses, and write the truths about our position before God and the truth of reconciliation:

> **Read John 3:15-18.**
>
> For God So Loved the World
> [16] "For God so loved the world,[b] that he gave his only Son, that whoever believes in him should not perish but have eternal life. [17] For God did not send his Son into the world to condemn the world, but in order that the world might be saved through him. [18] Whoever believes in him is not condemned, but whoever does not believe is condemned already, because he has not believed in the name of the only Son of God.

_____
_____
_____
_____
_____

LESSON 5:
WHAT IS RECONCILIATION? (PART 1)

> **Read John 5:24.**
>
> [24] Truly, truly, I say to you, whoever hears my word and believes him who sent me has eternal life. He does not come into judgment, but has passed from death to life.

_____
_____
_____
_____
_____

> **Read Colossians 1:9-23.**
>
> [9] And so, from the day we heard, we have not ceased to pray for you, asking that you may be filled with the knowledge of his will in all spiritual wisdom and understanding, [10] so as to walk in a manner worthy of the Lord, fully pleasing to him: bearing fruit in every good work and increasing in the knowledge of God; [11] being strengthened with all power, according to his glorious might, for all endurance and patience with joy; [12] giving thanks[a] to the Father, who has qualified you[b] to share in the inheritance of the saints in light. [13] He has delivered us from the domain of darkness and transferred us to the kingdom of his beloved Son, [14] in whom we have redemption, the forgiveness of sins.
>
> The Preeminence of Christ
>
> [15] He is the image of the invisible God, the firstborn of all creation. [16] For by[c] him all things were created, in heaven and on earth, visible and invisible, whether thrones or dominions or rulers or authorities—all things were created through him and for him. [17] And he is before all things, and in him all things hold together. [18] And he is the head of the body, the church. He is the beginning, the firstborn from the dead, that in everything he might be preeminent. [19] For in him all the fullness of God was pleased to dwell, [20] and through him to reconcile to himself all things, whether on earth or in heaven, making peace by the blood of his cross.

LESSON 5:
WHAT IS RECONCILIATION? (PART 1)

> ²¹ And you, who once were alienated and hostile in mind, doing evil deeds, ²² he has now reconciled in his body of flesh by his death, in order to present you holy and blameless and above reproach before him, ²³ if indeed you continue in the faith, stable and steadfast, not shifting from the hope of the gospel that you heard, which has been proclaimed in all creation[d] under heaven, and of which I, Paul, became a minister.

_____
_____
_____
_____
_____

Does Christ alter any of this truth to be reconciled to His created humans?
_____ (No)

Read these verses and write down the truth regarding the way to reconciliation to God:

> **Read John 14:6.**
>
> ⁶ Jesus said to him, "I am the way, and the truth, and the life. No one comes to the Father except through me.

_____
_____
_____
_____

LESSON 5:
WHAT IS RECONCILIATION? (PART 1)

> **Read John 3:36.**
>
> ³⁶ Whoever believes in the Son has eternal life; whoever does not obey the Son shall not see life, but the wrath of God remains on him.

_____
_____
_____
_____
_____

> **Read 1 John 5:12.**
>
> ¹² Whoever has the Son has life; whoever does not have the Son of God does not have life.

_____
_____
_____
_____
_____

Does Christ let us NOT be reconciled and eternally separated from Him, even though He has finished the work of forgiveness? _____ *(Yes)*

Why?

_____
_____
_____
_____
_____

LESSON 5:
WHAT IS RECONCILIATION? (PART 1)

What do these verses say about what Truth/Word will judge us? What does this mean about how we live and the truth about reconciliation?

> **Read Hebrews 4:11-13.**
>
> [11] Let us therefore strive to enter that rest, so that no one may fall by the same sort of disobedience. [12] For the word of God is living and active, sharper than any two-edged sword, piercing to the division of soul and of spirit, of joints and of marrow, and discerning the thoughts and intentions of the heart. [13] And no creature is hidden from his sight, but all are naked and exposed to the eyes of him to whom we must give account.

_____

_____

_____

_____

> **Read John 12:42-50.**
>
> [42] Nevertheless, many even of the authorities believed in him, but for fear of the Pharisees they did not confess it, so that they would not be put out of the synagogue; [43] for they loved the glory that comes from man more than the glory that comes from God.
>
> Jesus Came to Save the World
> [44] And Jesus cried out and said, "Whoever believes in me, believes not in me but in him who sent me. [45] And whoever sees me sees him who sent me. [46] I have come into the world as light, so that whoever believes in me may not remain in darkness. [47] If anyone hears my words and does not keep them, I do not judge him; for I did not come to judge the world but to save the world. [48] The one who rejects me and does not receive my words has a judge; the word that I have spoken will judge him on the last day. [49] For I have not spoken on my own authority, but the Father who sent me has himself given me a commandment—what to say and what to speak. [50] And I know that his commandment is eternal life. What I say, therefore, I say as the Father has told me."

LESSON 5:
WHAT IS RECONCILIATION? (PART 1)

_____
_____
_____
_____
_____

So, the gift of forgiveness must be believed in and then fully received and accepted in order for reconciliation and all of its benefits to be experienced. Again, the truth stands on its own. Christ has a heart and compassion for all to be reconciled to Him, just like 2 Peter 3:9 says:

> [9] The Lord is not slow to fulfill his promise as some count slowness, but is patient toward you,[a] not wishing that any should perish, but that all should reach repentance.

As believers, children of God, what does this mean to us?

If we have accepted Christ as our savior, can we be separated from Him again—not experiencing this fellowship? _____

Eternally? _____ *(No)*

What do these verses say about our eternal position once we have accepted Christ as our Lord and Savior?

> **Read John 5:24.**
>
> [24] Truly, truly, I say to you, whoever hears my word and believes him who sent me has eternal life. He does not come into judgment, but has passed from death to life.

LESSON 5:
WHAT IS RECONCILIATION? (PART 1)

_____
_____
_____
_____
_____

> **Read 1 John 5:11-12.**
>
> [11] And this is the testimony, that God gave us eternal life, and this life is in his Son. [12] Whoever has the Son has life; whoever does not have the Son of God does not have life.

_____
_____
_____
_____
_____

> **Read 1 Corinthians 3:11-15.**
>
> [11] For no one can lay a foundation other than that which is laid, which is Jesus Christ. [12] Now if anyone builds on the foundation with gold, silver, precious stones, wood, hay, straw— [13] each one's work will become manifest, for the Day will disclose it, because it will be revealed by fire, and the fire will test what sort of work each one has done. [14] If the work that anyone has built on the foundation survives, he will receive a reward. [15] If anyone's work is burned up, he will suffer loss, though he himself will be saved, but only as through fire.

Currently, in your daily living as a believer, are you experiencing His fellowship?

_____

LESSON 5:
WHAT IS RECONCILIATION? (PART 1)

The following verses explain what happens to believers who are not walking with God.

> **Read Romans 8:5-8.**
>
> ⁵ For those who live according to the flesh set their minds on the things of the flesh, but those who live according to the Spirit set their minds on the things of the Spirit. ⁶ For to set the mind on the flesh is death, but to set the mind on the Spirit is life and peace. ⁷ For the mind that is set on the flesh is hostile to God, for it does not submit to God's law; indeed, it cannot. ⁸ Those who are in the flesh cannot please God.

_____

_____

_____

_____

> **Read Psalm 78. (Read through the entire Psalm and write down the elements of sin that caused His children not to be reconciled to HIM.)**
>
> Tell the Coming Generation
> A Maskil[a] of Asaph.
> **78** Give ear, O my people, to my teaching;
>   incline your ears to the words of my mouth!
> ² I will open my mouth in a parable;
>   I will utter dark sayings from of old,
> ³ things that we have heard and known,
>   that our fathers have told us.
> ⁴ We will not hide them from their children,
>   but tell to the coming generation
> the glorious deeds of the Lord, and his might,
>   and the wonders that he has done.

LESSON 5:
WHAT IS RECONCILIATION? (PART 1)

> [5] He established a testimony in Jacob
>   and appointed a law in Israel,
> which he commanded our fathers
>   to teach to their children,
> [6] that the next generation might know them,
>   the children yet unborn,
> and arise and tell them to their children,
> [7] so that they should set their hope in God
> and not forget the works of God,
>   but keep his commandments;
> [8] and that they should not be like their fathers,
>   a stubborn and rebellious generation,
> a generation whose heart was not steadfast,
>   whose spirit was not faithful to God.
> [9] The Ephraimites, armed with[b] the bow,
>   turned back on the day of battle.
> [10] They did not keep God's covenant,
>   but refused to walk according to his law.
> [11] They forgot his works
>   and the wonders that he had shown them.
> [12] In the sight of their fathers he performed wonders
>   in the land of Egypt, in the fields of Zoan.
> [13] He divided the sea and let them pass through it,
>   and made the waters stand like a heap.
> [14] In the daytime he led them with a cloud,
>   and all the night with a fiery light.
> [15] He split rocks in the wilderness
>   and gave them drink abundantly as from the deep.
> [16] He made streams come out of the rock
>   and caused waters to flow down like rivers.
> [17] Yet they sinned still more against him,
>   rebelling against the Most High in the desert.
> [18] They tested God in their heart
>   by demanding the food they craved.
> [19] They spoke against God, saying,
>   "Can God spread a table in the wilderness?
> [20] He struck the rock so that water gushed out
>   and streams overflowed.

LESSON 5:
WHAT IS RECONCILIATION? (PART 1)

Can he also give bread
   or provide meat for his people?"
21 Therefore, when the Lord heard, he was full of wrath;
   a fire was kindled against Jacob;
   his anger rose against Israel,
22 because they did not believe in God
   and did not trust his saving power.
23 Yet he commanded the skies above
   and opened the doors of heaven,
24 and he rained down on them manna to eat
   and gave them the grain of heaven.
25 Man ate of the bread of the angels;
   he sent them food in abundance.
26 He caused the east wind to blow in the heavens,
   and by his power he led out the south wind;
27 he rained meat on them like dust,
   winged birds like the sand of the seas;
28 he let them fall in the midst of their camp,
   all around their dwellings.
29 And they ate and were well filled,
   for he gave them what they craved.
30 But before they had satisfied their craving,
   while the food was still in their mouths,
31 the anger of God rose against them,
   and he killed the strongest of them
   and laid low the young men of Israel.
32 In spite of all this, they still sinned;
   despite his wonders, they did not believe.
33 So he made their days vanish like[c] a breath,[d]
   and their years in terror.
34 When he killed them, they sought him;
   they repented and sought God earnestly.
35 They remembered that God was their rock,
   the Most High God their redeemer.
36 But they flattered him with their mouths;
   they lied to him with their tongues.
37 Their heart was not steadfast toward him;
   they were not faithful to his covenant.

LESSON 5:
WHAT IS RECONCILIATION? (PART 1)

³⁸ Yet he, being compassionate,
   atoned for their iniquity
   and did not destroy them;
he restrained his anger often
   and did not stir up all his wrath.
³⁹ He remembered that they were but flesh,
   a wind that passes and comes not again.
⁴⁰ How often they rebelled against him in the wilderness
   and grieved him in the desert!
⁴¹ They tested God again and again
   and provoked the Holy One of Israel.
⁴² They did not remember his power[e]
   or the day when he redeemed them from the foe,
⁴³ when he performed his signs in Egypt
   and his marvels in the fields of Zoan.
⁴⁴ He turned their rivers to blood,
   so that they could not drink of their streams.
⁴⁵ He sent among them swarms of flies, which devoured them,
   and frogs, which destroyed them.
⁴⁶ He gave their crops to the destroying locust
   and the fruit of their labor to the locust.
⁴⁷ He destroyed their vines with hail
   and their sycamores with frost.
⁴⁸ He gave over their cattle to the hail
   and their flocks to thunderbolts.
⁴⁹ He let loose on them his burning anger,
   wrath, indignation, and distress,
   a company of destroying angels.
⁵⁰ He made a path for his anger;
   he did not spare them from death,
   but gave their lives over to the plague.
⁵¹ He struck down every firstborn in Egypt,
   the firstfruits of their strength in the tents of Ham.
⁵² Then he led out his people like sheep
   and guided them in the wilderness like a flock.
⁵³ He led them in safety, so that they were not afraid,
   but the sea overwhelmed their enemies.
⁵⁴ And he brought them to his holy land,

LESSON 5:
WHAT IS RECONCILIATION? (PART 1)

> to the mountain which his right hand had won.
>
> 55 He drove out nations before them;
>   he apportioned them for a possession
>   and settled the tribes of Israel in their tents.
> 56 Yet they tested and rebelled against the Most High God
>   and did not keep his testimonies,
> 57 but turned away and acted treacherously like their fathers;
>   they twisted like a deceitful bow.
> 58 For they provoked him to anger with their high places;
>   they moved him to jealousy with their idols.
> 59 When God heard, he was full of wrath,
>   and he utterly rejected Israel.
> 60 He forsook his dwelling at Shiloh,
>   the tent where he dwelt among mankind,
> 61 and delivered his power to captivity,
>   his glory to the hand of the foe.
> 62 He gave his people over to the sword
>   and vented his wrath on his heritage.
> 63 Fire devoured their young men,
>   and their young women had no marriage song.
> 64 Their priests fell by the sword,
>   and their widows made no lamentation.
> 65 Then the Lord awoke as from sleep,
>   like a strong man shouting because of wine.
> 66 And he put his adversaries to rout;
>   he put them to everlasting shame.
> 67 He rejected the tent of Joseph;
>   he did not choose the tribe of Ephraim,
> 68 but he chose the tribe of Judah,
>   Mount Zion, which he loves.
> 69 He built his sanctuary like the high heavens,
>   like the earth, which he has founded forever.
> 70 He chose David his servant
>   and took him from the sheepfolds;
> 71 from following the nursing ewes he brought him
>   to shepherd Jacob his people,
>   Israel his inheritance.
> 72 With upright heart he shepherded them
>   and guided them with his skillful hand.

LESSON 5:
WHAT IS RECONCILIATION? (PART 1)

_____
_____
_____
_____
_____

Remember the questions in the previous section:

- Is there any way believers can be separated from God again?

- Can children of God be un-reconciled again and thus not experience His fellowship?

Eternally speaking, we now know, the answer is no. However, we must understand that we can experience separation from God's fellowship in the present.

> **Read Isaiah 59:1-4.**
>
> Evil and Oppression
> **59** Behold, the Lord's hand is not shortened, that it cannot save,
>   or his ear dull, that it cannot hear;
> ² but your iniquities have made a separation
>   between you and your God,
> and your sins have hidden his face from you
>   so that he does not hear.
> ³ For your hands are defiled with blood
>   and your fingers with iniquity;
> your lips have spoken lies;
>   your tongue mutters wickedness.
> ⁴ No one enters suit justly;
>   no one goes to law honestly;
> they rely on empty pleas, they speak lies,
>   they conceive mischief and give birth to iniquity.

LESSON 5:
WHAT IS RECONCILIATION? (PART 1)

Write down what you have learned about the truths of reconciliation and the implications for us to be reconciled with God and for us to reconcile with others.

_____
_____
_____
_____
_____

Since it is possible to not be reconciled with God, what is the remedy? Read these verses and write down the remedies:

> **Read 1 John 1:9.**
>
> [9] If we confess our sins, he is faithful and just to forgive us our sins and to cleanse us from all unrighteousness.

_____
_____
_____
_____

> **Read Psalm 51.**
>
> Create in Me a Clean Heart, O God
>
> To the choirmaster. A Psalm of David, when Nathan the prophet went to him, after he had gone in to Bathsheba.
>
> **51** Have mercy on me,[a] O God,
>   according to your steadfast love;
> according to your abundant mercy
>   blot out my transgressions.
> [2] Wash me thoroughly from my iniquity,

LESSON 5:
WHAT IS RECONCILIATION? (PART 1)

    and cleanse me from my sin!
³ For I know my transgressions,
    and my sin is ever before me.
⁴ Against you, you only, have I sinned
    and done what is evil in your sight,
so that you may be justified in your words
    and blameless in your judgment.
⁵ Behold, I was brought forth in iniquity,
    and in sin did my mother conceive me.
⁶ Behold, you delight in truth in the inward being,
    and you teach me wisdom in the secret heart.
⁷ Purge me with hyssop, and I shall be clean;
    wash me, and I shall be whiter than snow.
⁸ Let me hear joy and gladness;
    let the bones that you have broken rejoice.
⁹ Hide your face from my sins,
    and blot out all my iniquities.
¹⁰ Create in me a clean heart, O God,
    and renew a right[b] spirit within me.
¹¹ Cast me not away from your presence,
    and take not your Holy Spirit from me.
¹² Restore to me the joy of your salvation,
    and uphold me with a willing spirit.
¹³ Then I will teach transgressors your ways,
    and sinners will return to you.
¹⁴ Deliver me from bloodguiltiness, O God,
    O God of my salvation,
    and my tongue will sing aloud of your righteousness.
¹⁵ O Lord, open my lips,
    and my mouth will declare your praise.
¹⁶ For you will not delight in sacrifice, or I would give it;
    you will not be pleased with a burnt offering.
¹⁷ The sacrifices of God are a broken spirit;
    a broken and contrite heart, O God, you will not despise.
¹⁸ Do good to Zion in your good pleasure;
    build up the walls of Jerusalem;
¹⁹ then will you delight in right sacrifices,
    in burnt offerings and whole burnt offerings;
    then bulls will be offered on your altar.

LESSON 5:
WHAT IS RECONCILIATION? (PART 1)

Read 2 Chronicles 7:14-15.

¹⁴ if my people who are called by my name humble themselves, and pray and seek my face and turn from their wicked ways, then I will hear from heaven and will forgive their sin and heal their land. ¹⁵ Now my eyes will be open and my ears attentive to the prayer that is made in this place.

Read Deuteronomy 10:12-14.

Circumcise Your Heart
¹² "And now, Israel, what does the Lord your God require of you, but to fear the Lord your God, to walk in all his ways, to love him, to serve the Lord your God with all your heart and with all your soul, ¹³ and to keep the commandments and statutes of the Lord, which I am commanding you today for your good? ¹⁴ Behold, to the Lord your God belong heaven and the heaven of heavens, the earth with all that is in it.

LESSON 5:
WHAT IS RECONCILIATION? (PART 1)

_____
_____
_____
_____
_____

We learn here that we are to:

- Fear Him
- Walk in His ways
- Love Him with all heart and soul
- Serve Him
- Follow His instructions; surrender my will to His

What is the result?

_____
_____
_____
_____
_____

(Restored fellowship with Him)

Is this always available? _____ *(Yes)*

How many times can this happen? _____ *(Endlessly)*

> **Read Matthew 18:21-22.**
>
> The Parable of the Unforgiving Servant
> ²¹ Then Peter came up and said to him, "Lord, how often will my brother sin against me, and I forgive him? As many as seven times?" ²² Jesus said to him, "I do not say to you seven times, but seventy-seven times.

Does He alter the truth for us to experience this restoration?
_____ *(No)*

LESSON 5:
WHAT IS RECONCILIATION? (PART 1)

Experiencing Restoration

How does this relate to reconciliation? We recall that Christ never alters the truth in order for us to experience restoration and reconciliation. We can stay unreconciled and live outside of an intimate relationship with Him, outside of the benefits of living in this relationship.

> **Read Hebrews 3:15-19.**
>
> ^{15} As it is said,
>
> "Today, if you hear his voice,
> do not harden your hearts as in the rebellion."
>
> ^{16} For who were those who heard and yet rebelled? Was it not all those who left Egypt led by Moses? ^{17} And with whom was he provoked for forty years? Was it not with those who sinned, whose bodies fell in the wilderness? ^{18} And to whom did he swear that they would not enter his rest, but to those who were disobedient? ^{19} So we see that they were unable to enter because of unbelief.

Have you received this reconciliation from God? Are there others in your life you need to offer reconciliation to today? Remember, we are called to offer forgiveness to others as Christ offers forgiveness to the world—at all times and without condition. Regarding those who have hurt you, pray for God to give you the strength to forgive them, then forgive them. Do not allow your self-will to rule. Walk in God's Spirit and forgive them in His power, releasing them to God and then opening yourself up to absolute freedom with the Father.

_____
_____
_____
_____
_____
_____
_____
_____

LESSON 5:
WHAT IS RECONCILIATION? (PART 1)

LESSON 6:
WHAT IS RECONCILIATION? (PART 2)

What are the benefits of reconciliation? Read through the following verses and write out the wonderful benefits that we receive from being reconciled to Christ.

Redemption means that life is returned to us.

> **Read Ephesians 1:7-12.**
>
> 7 In him we have redemption through his blood, the forgiveness of our trespasses, according to the riches of his grace, 8 which he lavished upon us, in all wisdom and insight 9 making known[a] to us the mystery of his will, according to his purpose, which he set forth in Christ 10 as a plan for the fullness of time, to unite all things in him, things in heaven and things on earth.
>
> 11 In him we have obtained an inheritance, having been predestined according to the purpose of him who works all things according to the counsel of his will, 12 so that we who were the first to hope in Christ might be to the praise of his glory.

"When we allow God to pursue us, His life in us brings wholeness, fullness, and goodness."

_____
_____
_____
_____
_____
_____
_____
_____
_____
_____

LESSON 6:
WHAT IS RECONCILIATION? (PART 2)

> **Read 1 Corinthians 1:26-31.**
>
> 26 For consider your calling, brothers: not many of you were wise according to worldly standards,[a] not many were powerful, not many were of noble birth. 27 But God chose what is foolish in the world to shame the wise; God chose what is weak in the world to shame the strong; 28 God chose what is low and despised in the world, even things that are not, to bring to nothing things that are, 29 so that no human being[b] might boast in the presence of God. 30 And because of him[c] you are in Christ Jesus, who became to us wisdom from God, righteousness and sanctification and redemption, 31 so that, as it is written, "Let the one who boasts, boast in the Lord."

_____
_____
_____
_____
_____

When we allow God to pursue us, His life in us brings wholeness, fullness, and goodness.

Through His righteousness (and not our own), we are given the strength to pursue those things He has for us, especially, in this case, the power to move toward forgiveness and reconciliation. **Write for the following verses, God's work and invitation to receive freedom as we move forward.**

> **Read 1 John 1:9.**
>
> 9 If we confess our sins, he is faithful and just to forgive us our sins and to cleanse us from all unrighteousness.

_____
_____
_____
_____
_____

LESSON 6:
WHAT IS RECONCILIATION? (PART 2)

> **Read Romans 3:24-25.**
>
> ²⁴ and are justified by his grace as a gift, through the redemption that is in Christ Jesus,²⁵ whom God put forward as a propitiation by his blood, to be received by faith. This was to show God's righteousness, because in his divine forbearance he had passed over former sins.

_____
_____
_____
_____
_____

We cannot earn it or achieve it—just receive it and live in it.

> **Guidance: Read Psalm 32:8-9.**
>
> ⁸ I will instruct you and teach you in the way you should go;
>   I will counsel you with my eye upon you.
> ⁹ Be not like a horse or a mule, without understanding,
>   which must be curbed with bit and bridle,
>   or it will not stay near you.

_____
_____
_____
_____
_____

We have the privilege of having our lives directed by the sovereign God who knows all, has all power and might, and desires to give us the best!

LESSON 6:
WHAT IS RECONCILIATION? (PART 2)

> **Joy: Read Psalm 32:10-11.**
>
> [10] Many are the sorrows of the wicked,
>   but steadfast love surrounds the one who trusts in the Lord.
> [11] Be glad in the Lord, and rejoice, O righteous,
>   and shout for joy, all you upright in heart!

_____
_____
_____
_____
_____

We are given through God not worldly joy that is fleeting, but eternal, spiritual joy that fills our life with Him and the wonder and awe of daily walking with Him.

> **He forgets our failure: Read Psalm 103:12.**
>
> [12] as far as the east is from the west,
>   so far does he remove our transgressions from us.

_____
_____
_____
_____
_____

> **Read Hebrews 10:17.**
>
> [7] then he adds,
> "I will remember their sins and their lawless deeds no more."

LESSON 6:
WHAT IS RECONCILIATION? (PART 2)

_____
_____
_____
_____
_____

For the following verses write out the essence of our prayer as we receive God's supernatural work in the process of how we are proceed with reconciliation.

> **Power: Read Ephesians 1:15-23.**
>
> Thanksgiving and Prayer
> [15] For this reason, because I have heard of your faith in the Lord Jesus and your love[a] toward all the saints, [16] I do not cease to give thanks for you, remembering you in my prayers, [17] that the God of our Lord Jesus Christ, the Father of glory, may give you the Spirit of wisdom and of revelation in the knowledge of him, [18] having the eyes of your hearts enlightened, that you may know what is the hope to which he has called you, what are the riches of his glorious inheritance in the saints, [19] and what is the immeasurable greatness of his power toward us who believe, according to the working of his great might [20] that he worked in Christ when he raised him from the dead and seated him at his right hand in the heavenly places, [21] far above all rule and authority and power and dominion, and above every name that is named, not only in this age but also in the one to come. [22] And he put all things under his feet and gave him as head over all things to the church, [23] which is his body, the fullness of him who fills all in all.

_____
_____
_____
_____
_____

LESSON 6:
WHAT IS RECONCILIATION? (PART 2)

> **Read Ephesians 3:14-21.**
>
> Prayer for Spiritual Strength
> [14] For this reason I bow my knees before the Father, [15] from whom every family[a] in heaven and on earth is named, [16] that according to the riches of his glory he may grant you to be strengthened with power through his Spirit in your inner being, [17] so that Christ may dwell in your hearts through faith—that you, being rooted and grounded in love, [18] may have strength to comprehend with all the saints what is the breadth and length and height and depth, [19] and to know the love of Christ that surpasses knowledge, that you may be filled with all the fullness of God.
>
> [20] Now to him who is able to do far more abundantly than all that we ask or think, according to the power at work within us, [21] to him be glory in the church and in Christ Jesus throughout all generations, forever and ever. Amen.

_____
_____
_____
_____
_____

God desires to do supernatural things in our lives and in our circumstances and to demonstrate the wonder and awe of His power through us.

> **Peace: Read John 14:25-27.**
>
> [25] "These things I have spoken to you while I am still with you. [26] But the Helper, the Holy Spirit, whom the Father will send in my name, he will teach you all things and bring to your remembrance all that I have said to you. [27] Peace I leave with you; my peace I give to you. Not as the world gives do I give to you. Let not your hearts be troubled, neither let them be afraid.

LESSON 6:
WHAT IS RECONCILIATION? (PART 2)

Read Acts: 18-23. (When time allows, work through the stories of how Paul lived in complete peace despite all the interesting and difficult circumstances he faced. He completely trusted in and remained reconciled to God—all the time, every time.)

_____
_____
_____
_____
_____
_____
_____
_____
_____
_____

For the following verses, write out the benefits of receiving and thus living in forgiveness from God and thus having forgiveness for others and ourselves

> **Mercy, Kindness, and Tenderness: Read Psalm 103:4; 103:8-9.**
>
> ⁴ who redeems your life from the pit,
>   who crowns you with steadfast love and mercy,
>
> ⁸ The Lord is merciful and gracious,
>   slow to anger and abounding in steadfast love.
> ⁹ He will not always chide,
>   nor will he keep his anger forever.

_____
_____
_____
_____
_____

LESSON 6:
WHAT IS RECONCILIATION? (PART 2)

Read Psalm 130:7-8.

⁷ O Israel, hope in the Lord!
　For with the Lord there is steadfast love,
　　and with him is plentiful redemption.
⁸ And he will redeem Israel
　from all his iniquities.

_____
_____
_____
_____

Read Ephesians 4:31-32.

³¹ Let all bitterness and wrath and anger and clamor and slander be put away from you, along with all malice. ³² Be kind to one another, tenderhearted, forgiving one another, as God in Christ forgave you.

_____
_____
_____
_____

LESSON 6:
WHAT IS RECONCILIATION? (PART 2)

> **Healing: Read Psalm 103:3.**
>
> ³ who forgives all your iniquity,
>   who heals all your diseases…

_____
_____
_____
_____

> **Restored from destructive patterns: Read Psalm 103:4.**
>
> ⁴ who redeems your life from the pit,
> who crowns you with steadfast love and mercy…

_____
_____
_____
_____

LESSON 6:
WHAT IS RECONCILIATION? (PART 2)

> **To feel the satisfaction that comes with good things (renewal), read Psalm 103:5.**
>
> ⁵ who satisfies you with good
>   so that your youth is renewed like the eagle's.

Summary:

He desires to give us and have us experience good things in our lives. His best for us contributes to a life of freedom, joy, and peace.

Write down what you have learned about the truths of reconciliation, the benefits of reconciliation, and the implications for us to be reconciled with God and for us to reconcile with others.

LESSON 6:
WHAT IS RECONCILIATION? (PART 2)

Work through the following verses that help define the necessity of forgiveness and how we are to process reconciliation with others. What is the impact if we do not forgive?

Read Galatians 5:19-21.

[19] Now the works of the flesh are evident: sexual immorality, impurity, sensuality, [20] idolatry, sorcery, enmity, strife, jealousy, fits of anger, rivalries, dissensions, divisions, [21] envy,[a] drunkenness, orgies, and things like these. I warn you, as I warned you before, that those who do[b] such things will not inherit the kingdom of God.

_____
_____
_____
_____

Read Hebrews 12:14-17.

[14] Strive for peace with everyone, and for the holiness without which no one will see the Lord. [15] See to it that no one fails to obtain the grace of God; that no "root of bitterness" springs up and causes trouble, and by it many become defiled; [16] that no one is sexually immoral or unholy like Esau, who sold his birthright for a single meal. [17] For you know that afterward, when he desired to inherit the blessing, he was rejected, for he found no chance to repent, though he sought it with tears.

LESSON 6:
WHAT IS RECONCILIATION? (PART 2)

Read Galatians 5:1-6.

Christ Has Set Us Free
5 For freedom Christ has set us free; stand firm therefore, and do not submit again to a yoke of slavery.

² Look: I, Paul, say to you that if you accept circumcision, Christ will be of no advantage to you. ³ I testify again to every man who accepts circumcision that he is obligated to keep the whole law. ⁴ You are severed from Christ, you who would be justified[a] by the law; you have fallen away from grace. ⁵ For through the Spirit, by faith, we ourselves eagerly wait for the hope of righteousness. ⁶ For in Christ Jesus neither circumcision nor uncircumcision counts for anything, but only faith working through love.

Read Romans 1:24-32.

²⁴ Therefore God gave them up in the lusts of their hearts to impurity, to the dishonoring of their bodies among themselves, ²⁵ because they exchanged the truth about God for a lie and worshiped and served the creature rather than the Creator, who is blessed forever! Amen.

²⁶ For this reason God gave them up to dishonorable passions. For their women exchanged natural relations for those that are contrary to nature; ²⁷ and the men likewise gave up natural relations with women and were consumed with passion for one another, men committing shameless acts with men and receiving in themselves the due penalty for their error.

²⁸ And since they did not see fit to acknowledge God, God gave them up to a debased mind to do what ought not to be done. ²⁹ They were filled with all manner of unrighteousness, evil, covetousness, malice. They are full of envy, murder, strife, deceit, maliciousness. They are gossips, ³⁰ slanderers, haters of God, insolent, haughty, boastful, inventors of evil, disobedient to parents, ³¹ foolish, faithless, heartless, ruthless. ³² Though they know God's righteous decree that those who practice such things deserve to die, they not only do them but give approval to those who practice them.

LESSON 6:
WHAT IS RECONCILIATION? (PART 2)

> **How will we actually know we are living in forgiveness?**
> **Read Colossians 3:12-17.**
>
> [12] Put on then, as God's chosen ones, holy and beloved, compassionate hearts, kindness, humility, meekness, and patience, [13] bearing with one another and, if one has a complaint against another, forgiving each other; as the Lord has forgiven you, so you also must forgive. [14] And above all these put on love, which binds everything together in perfect harmony. [15] And let the peace of Christ rule in your hearts, to which indeed you were called in one body. And be thankful. [16] Let the word of Christ dwell in you richly, teaching and admonishing one another in all wisdom, singing psalms and hymns and spiritual songs, with thankfulness in your hearts to God. [17] And whatever you do, in word or deed, do everything in the name of the Lord Jesus, giving thanks to God the Father through him.

_____
_____
_____
_____

We will know we are in forgiveness when the thought of someone, or the name of someone mentioning that person, or having contact with someone do not bring us to anger, resentment, or a bitterness that brings us to a desire for withdrawal or revenge:

- We can be in same room as that person and remain in peace and freedom.

- We can intercede for that person, asking God for the best for that person.

LESSON 6:
WHAT IS RECONCILIATION? (PART 2)

Read 2 Timothy 2:20-26.

20 Now in a great house there are not only vessels of gold and silver but also of wood and clay, some for honorable use, some for dishonorable. 21 Therefore, if anyone cleanses himself from what is dishonorable,[a] he will be a vessel for honorable use, set apart as holy, useful to the master of the house, ready for every good work.

22 So flee youthful passions and pursue righteousness, faith, love, and peace, along with those who call on the Lord from a pure heart. 23 Have nothing to do with foolish, ignorant controversies; you know that they breed quarrels. 24 And the Lord's servant[b] must not be quarrelsome but kind to everyone, able to teach, patiently enduring evil, 25 correcting his opponents with gentleness. God may perhaps grant them repentance leading to a knowledge of the truth, 26 and they may come to their senses and escape from the snare of the devil, after being captured by him to do his will.

_____
_____
_____
_____
_____

Read Job 22:21-30.

21 "Agree with God, and be at peace;
   thereby good will come to you.
22 Receive instruction from his mouth,
   and lay up his words in your heart.
23 If you return to the Almighty you will be built up;
   if you remove injustice far from your tents,
24 if you lay gold in the dust,
   and gold of Ophir among the stones of the torrent-bed,
25 then the Almighty will be your gold
   and your precious silver.

LESSON 6:
WHAT IS RECONCILIATION? (PART 2)

> ²⁶ For then you will delight yourself in the Almighty
>   and lift up your face to God.
> ²⁷ You will make your prayer to him, and he will hear you,
>   and you will pay your vows.
> ²⁸ You will decide on a matter, and it will be established for you,
>   and light will shine on your ways.
> ²⁹ For when they are humbled you say, 'It is because of pride';[a]
>   but he saves the lowly.
> ³⁰ He delivers even the one who is not innocent,
>   who will be delivered through the cleanness of your hands."

At one of our retreats, we had a couple from out of town. Both the husband and the wife had been previously divorced and been married to each other for about 20 years. Thirty or so years earlier, the wife's ex-husband had kidnapped their daughter and moved to another state. The wife at the time did not have the wherewithal to pursue legal remedies and thus lost the ability to have a relationship with her daughter. In recent years, she was able to locate her daughter, now an adult, and made attempts to reconcile the relationship. Her daughter had been poisoned by her father. Because her thoughts about her mother had been horribly tainted by her father, she rebuffed any attempt to even talk together. She specifically requested that her mother leave her alone and never contact her again.

The wife held a deep level of bitterness toward her ex-husband and now toward her daughter who was not unwilling to open up even simple communications. The wife was living under additional pressure of disappointment and resignation (thinking that God was not really good), along with a level of guilt that she did not fight for her daughter when she was kidnapped. There were lots of emotions dominating her soul, resulting in a life of sadness and heaviness. During the retreat we addressed this whole issue of forgiveness and reconciliation: that God calls us to forgive 100 percent of the time and 100 percent of people, including those who have hurt us deeply. The wife recognized that this issue had put her in bondage and was the cause of her deep sadness. She spent time one afternoon in the Scriptures and in the Spirit, allowing God to transform her heart. She fully received His forgiveness and the ability to forgive both her ex-husband and her daughter. On the last day of the retreat she announced that she had experienced such freedom that she could intercede for both of them, that God would intervene in their lives to reveal to them each His forgiveness and thus a desire to reconcile the relationship of the daughter with her.

LESSON 6:
WHAT IS RECONCILIATION? (PART 2)

During her time of intercession, she heard God speak to her that He would bring about reconciliation with her daughter. The next day we received an incredible phone call. Having returned back home, the wife received a phone call from her daughter telling her that she had recently accepted Christ as Lord and Savior, and though she had struggled with her own issue of forgiveness and was not willing to even talk to her mother, God had broken through on Sunday and helped the daughter understand forgiveness. He gave her a desire to reconcile, that she was to call her mother to set up a time to meet and open the relationship. How cool is that? One of the beautiful truths of God is that He works both sides of every problem. This is one of the reasons we are to simply live in forgiveness, offer reconciliation, and allow God to do His work to bring about His desire for freedom and reconciled relationships. This was certainly a real example to all of us of the power of forgiveness and the beauty of reconciliation through forgiveness and intercession.

With this real story in mind, are there some painful and/or traumatic events in your past? Regardless of your involvement or guilt for lack of involvement, you might be in bondage to your bitterness and guilt just like this woman was. However, through forgiveness and allowing God to transform your heart, you can be released from all of your past hurts, even the excruciating events, and be set free. Are you willing to let God transform you from the inside out as well?

_____
_____
_____
_____
_____
_____
_____
_____
_____
_____
_____
_____
_____

LESSON 7:
AMBASSADORS IN RECONCILIATION

We are called to be ambassadors for Christ in His ministry of reconciliation. Read through these verses and then write how we are called to each.

Read Matthew 5:21-26.

Anger

21 "You have heard that it was said to those of old, 'You shall not murder; and whoever murders will be liable to judgment.' 22 But I say to you that everyone who is angry with his brother[a] will be liable to judgment; whoever insults[b] his brother will be liable to the council; and whoever says, 'You fool!' will be liable to the hell[c] of fire. 23 So if you are offering your gift at the altar and there remember that your brother has something against you, 24 leave your gift there before the altar and go. First be reconciled to your brother, and then come and offer your gift. 25 Come to terms quickly with your accuser while you are going with him to court, lest your accuser hand you over to the judge, and the judge to the guard, and you be put in prison. 26 Truly, I say to you, you will never get out until you have paid the last penny.[d]

"Those who have been reconciled are called, even ordered, to tell those who are not yet of God's flock about His forgiving nature, about His freely offered gift, about how to live in peace with their mighty and loving Creator."

LESSON 7:
AMBASSADORS IN RECONCILIATION

Read 2 Corinthians 5:12-21.

[12] We are not commending ourselves to you again but giving you cause to boast about us, so that you may be able to answer those who boast about outward appearance and not about what is in the heart. [13] For if we are beside ourselves, it is for God; if we are in our right mind, it is for you. [14] For the love of Christ controls us, because we have concluded this: that one has died for all, therefore all have died; [15] and he died for all, that those who live might no longer live for themselves but for him who for their sake died and was raised. [16] From now on, therefore, we regard no one according to the flesh. Even though we once regarded Christ according to the flesh, we regard him thus no longer. [17] Therefore, if anyone is in Christ, he is a new creation.[a] The old has passed away; behold, the new has come. [18] All this is from God, who through Christ reconciled us to himself and gave us the ministry of reconciliation; [19] that is, in Christ God was reconciling[b] the world to himself, not counting their trespasses against them, and entrusting to us the message of reconciliation. [20] Therefore, we are ambassadors for Christ, God making his appeal through us. We implore you on behalf of Christ, be reconciled to God. [21] For our sake he made him to be sin who knew no sin, so that in him we might become the righteousness of God.

_____
_____
_____
_____
_____

Read Hebrews 12:12-17.

[12] Therefore lift your drooping hands and strengthen your weak knees, [13] and make straight paths for your feet, so that what is lame may not be put out of joint but rather be healed. [14] Strive for peace with everyone, and for the holiness without which no one will see the Lord. [15] See to it that no one fails to obtain the grace of God; that no "root of bitterness" springs up and causes trouble, and by it many become defiled; [16] that no one is sexually immoral or unholy like

LESSON 7:
AMBASSADORS IN RECONCILIATION

> Esau, who sold his birthright for a single meal. [17]For you know that afterward, when he desired to inherit the blessing, he was rejected, for he found no chance to repent, though he sought it with tears.

_____
_____
_____
_____
_____

Read Romans 12:17-19.

[17] Repay no one evil for evil, but give thought to do what is honorable in the sight of all. [18] If possible, so far as it depends on you, live peaceably with all. [19] Beloved, never avenge yourselves, but leave it[a] to the wrath of God, for it is written, "Vengeance is mine, I will repay, says the Lord."

Read Psalm 34:11-22.

[11] Come, O children, listen to me;
   I will teach you the fear of the Lord.
[12] What man is there who desires life
   and loves many days, that he may see good?
[13] Keep your tongue from evil
   and your lips from speaking deceit.
[14] Turn away from evil and do good;
   seek peace and pursue it.
[15] The eyes of the Lord are toward the righteous
   and his ears toward their cry.
[16] The face of the Lord is against those who do evil,
   to cut off the memory of them from the earth.
[17] When the righteous cry for help, the Lord hears
   and delivers them out of all their troubles.

LESSON 7:
AMBASSADORS IN RECONCILIATION

> ¹⁸ The Lord is near to the brokenhearted
>   and saves the crushed in spirit.
> ¹⁹ Many are the afflictions of the righteous,
>   but the Lord delivers him out of them all.
> ²⁰ He keeps all his bones;
>   not one of them is broken.
> ²¹ Affliction will slay the wicked,
>   and those who hate the righteous will be condemned.
> ²² The Lord redeems the life of his servants;
>   none of those who take refuge in him will be condemned.

Read Psalm 25:4-5.

> ⁴ He who has clean hands and a pure heart,
>   who does not lift up his soul to what is false
>   and does not swear deceitfully.
> ⁵ He will receive blessing from the Lord
>   and righteousness from the God of his salvation.

_____
_____
_____
_____
_____

LESSON 7:
AMBASSADORS IN RECONCILIATION

> **Read Psalm 25:10.**
>
> 10 All the paths of the Lord are steadfast love and faithfulness,
>   for those who keep his covenant and his testimonies.

_____
_____
_____
_____

> **Read Ephesians 4:11-16; 4:25-27; 4:29-32.**
>
> 11 And he gave the apostles, the prophets, the evangelists, the shepherds[a] and teachers,[b] 12 to equip the saints for the work of ministry, for building up the body of Christ, 13 until we all attain to the unity of the faith and of the knowledge of the Son of God, to mature manhood,[c] to the measure of the stature of the fullness of Christ, 14 so that we may no longer be children, tossed to and fro by the waves and carried about by every wind of doctrine, by human cunning, by craftiness in deceitful schemes. 15 Rather, speaking the truth in love, we are to grow up in every way into him who is the head, into Christ, 16 from whom the whole body, joined and held together by every joint with which it is equipped, when each part is working properly, makes the body grow so that it builds itself up in love.
>
> 25 Therefore, having put away falsehood, let each one of you speak the truth with his neighbor, for we are members one of another. 26 Be angry and do not sin; do not let the sun go down on your anger, 27 and give no opportunity to the devil.
>
> 29 Let no corrupting talk come out of your mouths, but only such as is good for building up, as fits the occasion, that it may give grace to those who hear. 30 And do not grieve the Holy Spirit of God, by whom you were sealed for the day of redemption. 31 Let all bitterness and wrath and anger and clamor and slander be put away from you, along with all malice. 32 Be kind to one another, tenderhearted, forgiving one another, as God in Christ forgave you.

LESSON 7:
AMBASSADORS IN RECONCILIATION

> **Read Psalm 4:4-5.**
>
> [4] Be angry,[a] and do not sin;
>   ponder in your own hearts on your beds, and be silent. Selah
> [5] Offer right sacrifices,
>   and put your trust in the Lord.

> **Read Ephesians 4:32.**
>
> [32] Be kind to one another, tenderhearted, forgiving one another, as God in Christ forgave you.

LESSON 7:
AMBASSADORS IN RECONCILIATION

Read Ephesians 4:26-27.

26 Be angry and do not sin; do not let the sun go down on your anger, 27 and give no opportunity to the devil.

Read Luke 11:2-4.

2 And he said to them, "When you pray, say:
"Father, hallowed be your name.
Your kingdom come.
3 Give us each day our daily bread,[a]
4 and forgive us our sins,
   for we ourselves forgive everyone who is indebted to us.
And lead us not into temptation."

Philippians 2:1-11.

Christ's Example of Humility
2 So if there is any encouragement in Christ, any comfort from love, any participation in the Spirit, any affection and sympathy, 2 complete my joy by being of the same mind, having the same love, being in full accord and of one mind. 3 Do nothing from selfish ambition or conceit, but in humility count others more significant than yourselves. 4 Let each of you look not only to his own interests, but also to the interests of others. 5 Have this mind among yourselves, which is yours in Christ Jesus,[a] 6 who, though he was in the form of God, did not count equality with God a thing to be grasped,[b] 7 but emptied himself, by taking the form of a servant,[c] being born in the likeness of men. 8 And being found in human form, he humbled himself by becoming obedient to the point of death, even death on a cross. 9 Therefore God has highly exalted him and bestowed on him the name that is above every name, 10 so that at the name of Jesus every knee should bow, in heaven and on earth and under the earth, 11 and every tongue confess that Jesus Christ is Lord, to the glory of God the Father.

LESSON 7:
AMBASSADORS IN RECONCILIATION

> **Re-read Ephesians 4:25-32.**
>
> 25 Therefore, having put away falsehood, let each one of you speak the truth with his neighbor, for we are members one of another. 26 Be angry and do not sin; do not let the sun go down on your anger, 27 and give no opportunity to the devil. 28 Let the thief no longer steal, but rather let him labor, doing honest work with his own hands, so that he may have something to share with anyone in need. 29 Let no corrupting talk come out of your mouths, but only such as is good for building up, as fits the occasion, that it may give grace to those who hear. 30 And do not grieve the Holy Spirit of God, by whom you were sealed for the day of redemption. 31 Let all bitterness and wrath and anger and clamor and slander be put away from you, along with all malice. 32 Be kind to one another, tenderhearted, forgiving one another, as God in Christ forgave you.

If you find you are still emotionally angry and seeking revenge, this means you are not in forgiveness and are not able, in peace and freedom, to process the truth needed for reconciliation.

LESSON 7:
AMBASSADORS IN RECONCILIATION

If this is the case, then reevaluate:

- How does each see the truth about this situation?
- What resolutions does each have about this situation?
- Is there a resolution satisfactory to each party? Why or why not?
- How does each party see the truth about the situation at hand?
- What resolutions does each side offer regarding this situation?
- Is there a resolution which satisfies each party?
- If so, great! If not, why or why not?

At this point, the result is usually clear. Typically, the parties involved have either:

- processed the truth of the situation until there is agreement on the resolution so that reconciliation and a restored relationship ensues
- attempted to process the truth of the situation that cannot reach agreement on the resolution and remained either partially or completely un-reconciled
- they are not willing to process the truth at all and remained completely un-reconciled

The result will be clear:

Either you agree to be restored and reconciled, or you do not agree (still see things differently and no discussed resolution is satisfactory to either party), in which case there are three possibilities to come to reconciliation:

- My resolution is truth, and God has to change the other party's heart to understand and receive that truth.
- The other party's resolution is truth, and God has to change my heart to understand and receive that truth.
- God reveals a new resolution as He changes both parties' hearts to understand and receive this new truth.

This may take time, which is okay, as long as:

- We both are living in forgiveness.

LESSON 7:
AMBASSADORS IN RECONCILIATION

- We have listened, acknowledged, and clarified each other's view of truth.

- We continue to act with respect, kindness, and honor toward each other.

- Our lack of agreement does not ruin our day, our night, our weekend. We are able to set it aside and come back to it as we stay with it until agreement comes.

So, what is required for all this to work?

- Each party must first go to and remain in forgiveness.

- Each party must have a desire to be an ambassador for Christ and have a ministry of reconciliation.

- Each party must be willing to process truth—and have integrity about that truth.

- Each party must be willing to stay with the process until both an agreement and resolution become satisfactory to both.

- Now, if I am in forgiveness and fully willing for all this to work, the other party will set the level of reconciliation depending on their living in forgiveness and willingness to process truth. If there is:

- None, we will not be reconciled at all, and there will be no relationship, and will have separated.

- Partial, there will be a limited processing of truth, but an unwillingness to go to depth of the feelings of hurt experienced by me and see that what they have done has hurt and is unhealthy. At this, we cannot get to a full discussion of a resolution that is satisfactory to me since we never get to processing the full truth. This will result in a surface relationship, we will spend limited time together, and we will have boundaries regarding how much time and in what situations are satisfactory to and healthy for me.

- Complete, we will enjoy a fully restored relationship, with all the benefits of God's forgiveness.

- In order to process together to reach a resolution and reconciliation, the following tools are recommended:

LESSON 7:
AMBASSADORS IN RECONCILIATION

- How does each side see the truth about this situation? A good technique to use for this is to have each side share his/her view of what happened. After they have spoken, repeat what they have said and then ask, "Did I understand you correctly?" and "Is there anything else you would like to say regarding the issue?" Return to the beginning and repeat as many times as needed until both questions are answered positively, then reverse roles until you feel as though you have been fully heard and understood.

- Focus on the actual issue at hand. Once both sides have been fully heard and understood, often what happens is each party realizes they agree on more than they originally thought. Usually there is only one or two key issues needing to be resolved in the conflict. When you realize the actual issues, focus on those alone and work toward a resolution which will bring about reconciliation.

- Offer a solution. Once the key issues have been realized and discussed, each side should take a turn in offering a resolution satisfactory to both parties. First, the resolution would be stated and why it would be reasonable. Next, they would explain what they are willing to do (or not do, whatever the case may be) to resolve the issue. Then the opposing party would ask the same questions as before regarding the resolution, "Did I understand you correctly?" and "Is there anything else you would like to say here?" Once they are both positive answers, the other person takes a turn, just as before.

- Discuss if the solutions are acceptable to everyone. If they are, fantastic! Agree on the solution and live in the freedom of a reconciled and fully restored relationship, agreeing to not bring up the conflict again in the future. However, if neither resolution is adequate, more work needs to be done. Remember, the solution to the problem cannot violate Christ's truth. Therefore, the solutions must be truthful, and if they are not, then continue the process until they are. If a truthful resolution cannot be agreed upon, you must be willing to not be reconciled.

- The sooner we choose to process the truth, forgive, come to a resolution, and continue down the path toward full reconciliation, the sooner we will reap the benefits of walking in the Spirit: peace that passes all understanding and the freedom that truly sets us free. However, going through the entire process may take some time, which is completely understandable and acceptable. Our role is to make sure that we are living in forgiveness and let God speak to the other side.

LESSON 7:
AMBASSADORS IN RECONCILIATION

Also, make sure you are listening to the other party's side, clarifying along the way as needed, all the while acknowledging their feelings and words and view of the truth. In addition, ensure to continue acting with respect, kindness, and honor toward our offender. However, if you are not being treated with respect and honor, the process may have to cease until respect can be shown on both sides or both parties will have to live unreconciled. If this is being threatened, ask yourself and your offender if you both can set aside the conflict until a later date, but with a continued heart toward resolution. With these attitudes and guidelines practiced, we should be able to live in such a way that a lack of agreement does not ruin our attitudes, our days and nights, our interactions with others. For this to work fully, a few things must happen on both sides of the conflict:

- Each party must turn first to forgiveness and remain in forgiveness. If you are operating in forgiveness but your offender is not, keep the forgiving mindset. If believers continue to walk guided by the Spirit and remain humble, it creates an environment where it is easier for the other party to process with respect, kindness, and honor.

- Each party must have a desire to be an ambassador for Christ and have a ministry of reconciliation. Again, we are only responsible for ourselves. If the opposing person or party has no desire to participate in the ministry of reconciliation, we are to remain being ambassadors and continue treating them with respect. The offer to process through the conflict is presented over and over with respect. Each party must be willing to process the truth of the situation and have integrity while doing it.

- Each party must be willing to process truth—and have integrity about that truth. You need to continually stand on the truth, share the truth, and never compromise the truth. Just as important is for you to ask the other person(s) to stand on their truth, share their truth, and not compromise their truth. Why? You do not want the other party to give in or cave merely for the sake of resolving or avoiding conflict. When this happens, conflicts are never resolved. Because of this, you need to create a safe environment for them to continue to share what's on their heart so that a resolution based around truth is truly reached. This is particularly significant for a couple where one party generally will give in just to avoid the conflict. Work hard at this, and you will see the ability to process truth well will lead to wonderful resolutions and the fulfillment of God's will.

LESSON 7:
AMBASSADORS IN RECONCILIATION

- Each party must be willing to stay within the process until an agreement is found and a resolution suitable for both parties is decided. As far as it concerns you, you should always be willing to continue the reconciliation process. The other party, due to their lack of forgiveness and bondage to their own soul wounds, may walk away from the process and refuse to process further. Remember, your call is to forgive at all times but that reconciliation is based upon truth. You cannot control the other party's response to that truth. So, if they are not willing to be reconciled, then you have to be willing to let the relationship be unreconciled but always having the freedom in forgiveness and a willingness to process again if the other party ever decides they desire to pursue truth with you.

As we serve as ambassadors in this ministry of reconciliation, we and the other party experience wonderful benefits:

- Redemption (we receive life back)
- His righteousness
- Guidance
- Joy
- He forgets our failure
- Spiritual power and authority
- Peace
- Mercy, kindness, and tenderness
- Healing
- Restoration from destructive patterns
- Satisfaction with good things (renewal)

As you allow the Holy Spirit to transform your mind, your heart, your life, you will greatly reap all of the benefits of living in the Kingdom and that life will be everything you have ever wanted, dared to dream of, and more. The choice is yours, and the call to follow Christ in forgiveness and reconciliation is always available to you. Leave behind your past failures, your former pain, and look forward and upward. The questions asked to you from your Heavenly Father are simply and always this:

Why not today? Why not now?

LESSON 7:
AMBASSADORS IN RECONCILIATION

Write down what you have learned about the truths of forgiveness and reconciliation, and the implications for us to be reconciled with God and for us to reconcile with others.

LESSON 8:
PRACTICAL WAYS OF RECONCILIATION IN A VARIETY OF SITUATIONS

> "When we pray for non-believers to respond to God's truth, which offers eternal redemption and restoration, we are near the very heart of God."

Work through the following situations that impact our ability to reconcile. Review the verses and write out what they are speaking to you.

1. **What about justice? Does the other party deserve justice when in fact, they did wrong and were completely unfair, their deed being a true injustice?**

Re-read Romans 12:9-21.

Marks of the True Christian
[9] Let love be genuine. Abhor what is evil; hold fast to what is good. [10] Love one another with brotherly affection. Outdo one another in showing honor. [11] Do not be slothful in zeal, be fervent in spirit,[a] serve the Lord. [12] Rejoice in hope, be patient in tribulation, be constant in prayer. [13] Contribute to the needs of the saints and seek to show hospitality.

[14] Bless those who persecute you; bless and do not curse them. [15] Rejoice with those who rejoice, weep with those who weep. [16] Live in harmony with one another. Do not be haughty, but associate with the lowly.[b] Never be wise in your own sight. [17] Repay no one evil for evil, but give thought to do what is honorable in the sight of all. [18] If possible, so far as it depends on you, live peaceably with all. [19] Beloved, never avenge yourselves, but leave it[c] to the wrath of God, for it is written, "Vengeance is mine, I will repay, says the Lord." [20] To the contrary, "if your enemy is hungry, feed him; if he is thirsty, give him something to drink; for by so doing you will heap burning coals on his head." [21] Do not be overcome by evil, but overcome evil with good.

_____
_____
_____
_____
_____

LESSON 8:
PRACTICAL WAYS OF RECONCILIATION IN A VARIETY OF SITUATIONS

These verses call us toward:

- Forgiveness
- Kindness, respect, honor
- Replacing good for evil
- Believing that the injustice will be corrected. Justice will prevail; and revenge is up to God to fulfill (have to have long view of it), not me. I can let it go.

2. What about those who have passed away with no chance for reconciliation?

> **Read Isaiah 61:1-4; Psalm 103:1-5.**
>
> The Year of the Lord's Favor
> **61** The Spirit of the Lord God is upon me,
>   because the Lord has anointed me
> to bring good news to the poor;[a]
>   he has sent me to bind up the brokenhearted,
> to proclaim liberty to the captives,
>   and the opening of the prison to those who are bound;[b]
> ² to proclaim the year of the Lord's favor,
>   and the day of vengeance of our God;
>   to comfort all who mourn;
> ³ to grant to those who mourn in Zion—
>   to give them a beautiful headdress instead of ashes,
> the oil of gladness instead of mourning,
>   the garment of praise instead of a faint spirit;
> that they may be called oaks of righteousness,
>   the planting of the Lord, that he may be glorified.[c]
> ⁴ They shall build up the ancient ruins;
>   they shall raise up the former devastations;
> they shall repair the ruined cities,
>   the devastations of many generations.

LESSON 8:
PRACTICAL WAYS OF RECONCILIATION IN A VARIETY OF SITUATIONS

> **Bless the Lord, O My Soul**
>
> Of David.
> **103** Bless the Lord, O my soul,
>   and all that is within me,
>   bless his holy name!
> ² Bless the Lord, O my soul,
>   and forget not all his benefits,
> ³ who forgives all your iniquity,
>   who heals all your diseases,
> ⁴ who redeems your life from the pit,
>   who crowns you with steadfast love and mercy,
> ⁵ who satisfies you with good
>   so that your youth is renewed like the eagle's.

_____
_____
_____
_____
_____

3. **What about the mother and/or father who have deeply abused or hurt me; and who my still be hurting me?**

   - Remember forgiveness

   - Remember the command to honor that comes with a promise of blessing or curse.

> **Read Exodus 20:12; Ephesians 6:2.**
>
> ¹² "Honor your father and your mother, that your days may be long in the land that the Lord your God is giving you.
>
> ² "Honor your father and mother" (this is the first commandment with a promise).

LESSON 8:
PRACTICAL WAYS OF RECONCILIATION IN A VARIETY OF SITUATIONS

_____
_____
_____
_____
_____

How? Though they may not be willing to process any truth, our role is to move the level of reconciliation from none to partial. Here you are to:

- Be willing to have a surface relationship

- Offer respect, kindness, honor

- Establish healthy boundaries while maintaining honor;

  - Pray for protection of heart

  - Practice avoiding getting drawn into unhealthy situations and responding when buttons are pushed

  - If limited time, remember it is for a short time and can be released.

Read Deuteronomy 30:15-20.

[15] "See, I have set before you today life and good, death and evil. [16] If you obey the commandments of the Lord your God[a] that I command you today, by loving the Lord your God, by walking in his ways, and by keeping his commandments and his statutes and his rules,[b] then you shall live and multiply, and the Lord your God will bless you in the land that you are entering to take possession of it. [17] But if your heart turns away, and you will not hear, but are drawn away to worship other gods and serve them, [18] I declare to you today, that you shall surely perish. You shall not live long in the land that you are going over the Jordan to enter and possess. [19] I call heaven and earth to witness against you today, that I have set before you life and death, blessing and curse. Therefore, choose life, that you and your offspring may live, [20] loving the Lord your God, obeying his voice and holding fast to him, for he is your life and length of days, that you may dwell in the land that the Lord swore to your fathers, to Abraham, to Isaac, and to Jacob, to give them."

LESSON 8:
PRACTICAL WAYS OF RECONCILIATION IN A VARIETY OF SITUATIONS

4. What about a person who has cut me off?

Read John 6:53-67; Luke 18:18-30.

[53] So Jesus said to them, "Truly, truly, I say to you, unless you eat the flesh of the Son of Man and drink his blood, you have no life in you. [54] Whoever feeds on my flesh and drinks my blood has eternal life, and I will raise him up on the last day. [55] For my flesh is true food, and my blood is true drink. [56] Whoever feeds on my flesh and drinks my blood abides in me, and I in him. [57] As the living Father sent me, and I live because of the Father, so whoever feeds on me, he also will live because of me. [58] This is the bread that came down from heaven, not like the bread[a] the fathers ate, and died. Whoever feeds on this bread will live forever." [59] Jesus[b] said these things in the synagogue, as he taught at Capernaum.

The Words of Eternal Life
[60] When many of his disciples heard it, they said, "This is a hard saying; who can listen to it?" [61] But Jesus, knowing in himself that his disciples were grumbling about this, said to them, "Do you take offense at this? [62] Then what if you were to see the Son of Man ascending to where he was before? [63] It is the Spirit who gives life; the flesh is no help at all. The words that I have spoken to you are spirit and life. [64] But there are some of you who do not believe."(For Jesus knew from the beginning who those were who did not believe, and who it was who would betray him.) [65] And he said, "This is why I told you that no one can come to me unless it is granted him by the Father."

[66] After this many of his disciples turned back and no longer walked with him. [67] So Jesus said to the twelve, "Do you want to go away as well?"

The Rich Ruler
[18] And a ruler asked him, "Good Teacher, what must I do to inherit eternal life?" [19] And Jesus said to him, "Why do you call me good? No one is good except God alone. [20] You know the commandments: 'Do not commit adultery, Do not murder, Do not steal, Do not bear false witness, Honor your father and mother.'" [21] And he said, "All these I have kept from my youth." [22] When Jesus heard this, he said to him, "One thing you still lack. Sell all that you have and distribute to the poor, and you will have treasure in heaven; and come, follow me." [23] But when he heard these things, he became very sad, for he was

LESSON 8:
PRACTICAL WAYS OF RECONCILIATION IN A VARIETY OF SITUATIONS

> extremely rich. ²⁴ Jesus, seeing that he had become sad, said, "How difficult it is for those who have wealth to enter the kingdom of God! ²⁵ For it is easier for a camel to go through the eye of a needle than for a rich person to enter the kingdom of God." ²⁶ Those who heard it said, "Then who can be saved?" ²⁷ But he said, "What is impossible with man is possible with God." ²⁸ And Peter said, "See, we have left our homes and followed you." ²⁹ And he said to them, "Truly, I say to you, there is no one who has left house or wife or brothers[a] or parents or children, for the sake of the kingdom of God, ³⁰ who will not receive many times more in this time, and in the age to come eternal life."

_____
_____
_____
_____
_____

- Go to forgiveness

- Offer reconciliation. Meet to discuss so you can apologize for anything you have done and discuss things openly. Then follow the rest of process. If they refuse, then you can live in forgiveness, in freedom, and always willing to immediately begin the process of reconciliation if and when the other party is ready.

- Continue respect, kindness, and honor whenever we see the other person or are in their presence.

> **Read Luke 10:1-16.**
>
> Jesus Sends Out the Seventy-Two
> **10** After this the Lord appointed seventy-two[a] others and sent them on ahead of him, two by two, into every town and place where he himself was about to go. ² And he said to them, "The harvest is plentiful, but the laborers are few. Therefore pray earnestly to the Lord of the harvest to send out laborers into his harvest. ³ Go your way; behold, I am sending you out as lambs in the midst

LESSON 8:
PRACTICAL WAYS OF RECONCILIATION IN A VARIETY OF SITUATIONS

> of wolves. ⁴Carry no moneybag, no knapsack, no sandals, and greet no one on the road. ⁵Whatever house you enter, first say, 'Peace be to this house!' ⁶And if a son of peace is there, your peace will rest upon him. But if not, it will return to you. ⁷And remain in the same house, eating and drinking what they provide, for the laborer deserves his wages. Do not go from house to house. ⁸Whenever you enter a town and they receive you, eat what is set before you. ⁹Heal the sick in it and say to them, 'The kingdom of God has come near to you.' ¹⁰But whenever you enter a town and they do not receive you, go into its streets and say, ¹¹'Even the dust of your town that clings to our feet we wipe off against you. Nevertheless know this, that the kingdom of God has come near.' ¹²I tell you, it will be more bearable on that day for Sodom than for that town.
>
> Woe to Unrepentant Cities
> ¹³"Woe to you, Chorazin! Woe to you, Bethsaida! For if the mighty works done in you had been done in Tyre and Sidon, they would have repented long ago, sitting in sackcloth and ashes. ¹⁴But it will be more bearable in the judgment for Tyre and Sidon than for you. ¹⁵And you, Capernaum, will you be exalted to heaven? You shall be brought down to Hades.
>
> ¹⁶"The one who hears you hears me, and the one who rejects you rejects me, and the one who rejects me rejects him who sent me."

5. **What about the person who says they are willing to talk, but are never willing to admit and deal with what they have done to hurt me (denial and rationalization)?**

Though they may not be willing to process any truth, our role is to move the level of reconciliation from none to partial. You will need to:

- Be willing to have a surface relationship
- Offer respect, kindness, honor
- Establish healthy boundaries while maintaining honor;
    - Pray for protection of their heart
    - Practice avoiding getting drawn into unhealthy situations and responding when buttons are pushed
    - If limited time, remember this is for a short time and eventually can release it all.

LESSON 8:
PRACTICAL WAYS OF RECONCILIATION IN A VARIETY OF SITUATIONS

Even though they may not be willing to process any truth, our role is still to move the level of reconciliation from a severed relationship to a partial one, as much as it relies upon us. Just as when we were discussing parents, we must be willing to have only a surface relationship while continuing to treat them with respect, kindness, and honor. Remember, establishing healthy boundaries can be accomplished by:

- Praying for the protection of our heart
- Practicing avoidance when it comes to getting drawn into unhealthy situations
- Avoiding response when our "hot buttons" are pushed
- Reminding yourself that it is only for a short time (if there is a time limit) and the release will come when the time is over.

6. How do I let myself off the hook?

- Forgiveness on the same basis as above
- Reconciliation to God's truth

> **Read Romans 8:1-2.**
>
> Life in the Spirit
> **8** There is therefore now no condemnation for those who are in Christ Jesus.[a] 2 For the law of the Spirit of life has set you[b] free in Christ Jesus from the law of sin and death.

_____
_____
_____
_____

LESSON 8:
PRACTICAL WAYS OF RECONCILIATION IN A VARIETY OF SITUATIONS

Remember all the truths and benefits listed above, particularly forgetting and redemption.

> **Read Philippians 3:12-16.**
>
> Straining Toward the Goal
> ¹² Not that I have already obtained this or am already perfect, but I press on to make it my own, because Christ Jesus has made me his own. ¹³ Brothers, I do not consider that I have made it my own. But one thing I do: forgetting what lies behind and straining forward to what lies ahead, ¹⁴ I press on toward the goal for the prize of the upward call of God in Christ Jesus. ¹⁵ Let those of us who are mature think this way, and if in anything you think otherwise, God will reveal that also to you. ¹⁶ Only let us hold true to what we have attained.

_____
_____
_____
_____
_____

> **Read Romans 8:38-39 (does not mention past).**
>
> ³⁸ For I am sure that neither death nor life, nor angels nor rulers, nor things present nor things to come, nor powers, ³⁹ nor height nor depth, nor anything else in all creation, will be able to separate us from the love of God in Christ Jesus our Lord.

_____
_____
_____
_____
_____

LESSON 8:
PRACTICAL WAYS OF RECONCILIATION IN A VARIETY OF SITUATIONS

To process truth:

- Is reconciliation needed?

- Is restitution needed?

- Do we need to let go of the past, release, live in truth of God's forgiveness and move on to high calling of Christ Jesus? Yes!

7. **What about marriage: What is our call to reconcile?**

Marriage is the only relationship where we are called to reconcile all the time, every time, 100 percent of the time. We are commanded to live in complete unity.

> **Read Psalm 133.**
>
> When Brothers Dwell in Unity
> A Song of Ascents. Of David.
> **133** Behold, how good and pleasant it is
>   when brothers dwell in unity![a]
> ² It is like the precious oil on the head,
>   running down on the beard,
> on the beard of Aaron,
>   running down on the collar of his robes!
> ³ It is like the dew of Hermon,
>   which falls on the mountains of Zion!
> For there the Lord has commanded the blessing,
>   life forevermore.

_____
_____
_____
_____

LESSON 8:
PRACTICAL WAYS OF RECONCILIATION IN A VARIETY OF SITUATIONS

> **Read Psalm 128.**
>
> Blessed Is Everyone Who Fears the Lord
> A Song of Ascents.
> **128** Blessed is everyone who fears the Lord,
>   who walks in his ways!
> ² You shall eat the fruit of the labor of your hands;
>   you shall be blessed, and it shall be well with you.
> ³ Your wife will be like a fruitful vine
>   within your house;
> your children will be like olive shoots
>   around your table.
> ⁴ Behold, thus shall the man be blessed
>   who fears the Lord.
> ⁵ The Lord bless you from Zion!
>   May you see the prosperity of Jerusalem
>   all the days of your life!
> ⁶ May you see your children's children!
>   Peace be upon Israel!

_____
_____
_____
_____
_____

> **Read Ecclesiastes 9:7-10.**
> **Enjoy Life with the One You Love**
>
> ⁷ Go, eat your bread with joy, and drink your wine with a merry heart, for God has already approved what you do.
>
> ⁸ Let your garments be always white. Let not oil be lacking on your head.

LESSON 8:
PRACTICAL WAYS OF RECONCILIATION IN A VARIETY OF SITUATIONS

> [9] Enjoy life with the wife whom you love, all the days of your vain[a] life that he has given you under the sun, because that is your portion in life and in your toil at which you toil under the sun. [10] Whatever your hand finds to do, do it with your might,[b] for there is no work or thought or knowledge or wisdom in Sheol, to which you are going.

_____
_____
_____
_____

> **Read Ecclesiastes 4:9-12.**
>
> [9] Two are better than one, because they have a good reward for their toil. [10] For if they fall, one will lift up his fellow. But woe to him who is alone when he falls and has not another to lift him up! [11] Again, if two lie together, they keep warm, but how can one keep warm alone? [12] And though a man might prevail against one who is alone, two will withstand him—a threefold cord is not quickly broken.

_____
_____
_____
_____
_____

LESSON 8:
PRACTICAL WAYS OF RECONCILIATION IN A VARIETY OF SITUATIONS

> **Read Philippians 2:1-4.**
> **Christ's Example of Humility**
>
> **2** So if there is any encouragement in Christ, any comfort from love, any participation in the Spirit, any affection and sympathy, ² complete my joy by being of the same mind, having the same love, being in full accord and of one mind. ³ Do nothing from selfish ambition or conceit, but in humility count others more significant than yourselves. ⁴ Let each of you look not only to his own interests, but also to the interests of others.

_____
_____
_____
_____
_____

> **Read Ephesians 4:1-6.**
> **Unity in the Body of Christ**
>
> **4** I therefore, a prisoner for the Lord, urge you to walk in a manner worthy of the calling to which you have been called, ² with all humility and gentleness, with patience, bearing with one another in love, ³ eager to maintain the unity of the Spirit in the bond of peace. ⁴ There is one body and one Spirit—just as you were called to the one hope that belongs to your call—⁵ one Lord, one faith, one baptism, ⁶ one God and Father of all, who is over all and through all and in all.

_____
_____
_____
_____

www.ingramcontent.com/pod-product-compliance
Lightning Source LLC
Chambersburg PA
CBHW051257110526
44589CB00025B/2857